D0987188

A Da Capo Press Reprint Series

THE AMERICAN SCENE
Comments and Commentators

GENERAL EDITOR: WALLACE D. FARNHAM
University of Illinois

THE COURTS THE CONSTITUTION AND PARTIES

STUDIES IN CONSTITUTIONAL HISTORY AND POLITICS

By Andrew C. McLaughlin

DA CAPO PRESS • NEW YORK • 1972

Library of Congress Cataloging in Publication Data

McLaughlin, Andrew Cunningham, 1861-1947.
The courts, the Constitution, and parties.

(The American scene: comments and commentators)
Reprint of the 1912 ed.
1. Courts—United States. 2. United States—Constitutional history. 3. United States—Politics and government. I. Title.
JK1541.M3 1972 320.9'73 70-87405
ISBN 0-306-71549-X

This Da Capo Press edition of *The Courts, The Constitution and Parties* is an unabridged republication of the first edition published in Chicago in 1912. It is reprinted with permission from a copy of the original edition in the collection of the Alderman Library, University of Virginia.

Published by Da Capo Press, Inc.
A Subsidiary of Plenum Publishing Corporation
227 West 17th Street, New York, New York 10011

Manufactured in the United States of America

THE COURTS, THE CONSTITUTION AND PARTIES

THE UNIVERSITY OF CHICAGO PRESS
CHICAGO, ILLINOIS

Agents
THE BAKER & TAYLOR COMPANY
NEW YORK

THE CAMBRIDGE UNIVERSITY PRESS
LONDON AND EDINBURGH

THE COURTS THE CONSTITUTION AND PARTIES

STUDIES IN CONSTITUTIONAL HISTORY AND POLITICS

By

ANDREW C. McLAUGHLIN

Professor of History in the University of Chicago

THE UNIVERSITY OF CHICAGO PRESS
CHICAGO, ILLINOIS

Published August 1912

Composed and Printed By
The University of Chicago Press
Chicago, Illinois, U.S.A.

PREFACE

The author of this volume believes that it includes a discussion of cardinal principles and facts in American constitutional history. The first article deals with the origin of the principle that courts can declare laws void. The second and third treat of the vital institutions, which, though not recognized by written constitutions, came into existence as opportunity was offered to realize popular government; within themselves political parties embodied the problem of popular government, for, if the people could not control the party management or the "organization," they could not make their own desires effective. The fourth article discusses the changing theories of political philosophy, which, as the years went by, furnished foundations for differing theories concerning the nature of the Union. The fifth shows that American legal order took its rise in the theory of compact and of individual right and in the belief that imperial order itself should rest on law—two theories or principles that now confront the reformer seeking to readjust social systems and to make them conform to what he considers present social demands.

All except the first, the longest of these papers, have appeared elsewhere in print. I hope the republication is justified by their value and interest and by the fact that the five papers in combination constitute a discussion of the most fundamental problems of constitutional history. The paper on "The Significance of Political Parties" appeared in the *Atlantic Monthly* and is here reprinted with the courteous permission of the publishers of that magazine. The paper on "Political Parties and Popular Government" was given as an address before the Phi Beta Kappa Society of Indiana University in June, 1911. "Social Compact and Constitutional Construction" was printed in the *American Historical Review*. The last paper was printed in the Michigan *Law Review* and in the *Proceedings of the Fiftieth Anniversary of the Constitution of Iowa*. I wish to express my appreciation of the assistance of one of my students, Mr. Arthur P. Scott, in the search for the early court decisions, which either involved the principle that laws may be declared void or stated principles of political philosophy.

A. C. McL.

CHICAGO
August 1, 1912

TABLE OF CONTENTS

I. THE POWER OF A COURT TO DECLARE A LAW UNCONSTITUTIONAL

THE POWER OF A COURT TO DECLARE A LAW UNCONSTITUTIONAL

A SURVEY OF THE HISTORICAL BACKGROUND[1]

In our political and partisan discussions of the present day we appear to be much concerned with the power and the tendencies of the courts. Of particular interest to students of politics and to practical politicians alike is the power of the courts to declare a law unconstitutional. The reason for this interest and for the political problem involved is not far to seek and is so well known that it is not necessary here to give the subject more than a passing word. We have in recent years passed into a new stage of industrial and social being; we have changed our business methods and our habits of mind; we have outgrown in business activity and in social sentiment the conditions of individualism that were dominant in the early days of the Republic and for decades thereafter; we are face to face with the fact that society has duties

[1] A portion of this paper was delivered as a presidential address before the Mississippi Valley Historical Association, May 23, 1912.

and responsibilities and that any principles which set up isolated individual right as over against community interest are at least fraught with danger, if they are not pure anachronisms; we have come to the time when men believe that a good government is one that can do things and will do things, and not merely refrain from doing things. In this changing order the courts have been tested to the utmost; the ingenuity of judges has been strained in efforts to accommodate the law, and inherited principles of individual right under the law, to the demands for the recognition of social justice. This whole discussion is fundamental and of deepest importance, arising, not from any mere passing ferment on a trivial matter, but from a consideration of vital needs in the state.

The power of the federal Supreme Court to declare a law of Congress unconstitutional has of late been receiving special attention from students of history and politics. A number of able articles have been written on both sides of this question.[1] The intent of this paper is

[1] Some of the more important treatments are found in J. B. Thayer, *Cases on Constitutional Law*, I; J. B. Thayer, *Legal Essays*, C. H. McIlwain, *The High Court of Parliament and Its Supremacy;* C. A. Beard, "The Supreme Court, Usurper or Grantee," *Pol. Sci. Quart.*, XXVII (March, 1912); Brinton Coxe, *Judicial Power and Unconstitutional Legislation;* Austin

not to show that the Supreme Court usurped authority in 1803 when Marshall declared a portion of the Judiciary Act invalid or to prove, on the other hand, that the power exercised by Marshall was clearly within the authority of the court; my intention is rather to trace in a broad and general way the historical facts and forces which preceded that decision; to give as far as possible in a few words the historical background, which will explain, if it does not justify, the position of the court. For, whatever may be the number of court decisions which might be referred to as technical precedents, the historical student, with the perversity characteristic of historical inquiry, desires to know whence came these court decisions or

Scott, "*Holmes* vs. *Walton*, the New Jersey Precedent," *Am. Hist. Rev.*, IV, 456; Chief Justice Walter Clark of North Carolina, address before Law Department of University of Pennsylvania, reprinted in *Congressional Record*, August 4, 1911; W. M. Meigs, "Independence of Departments of Government," *Am. Law Rev.*, XXIII, 594; W. M. Meigs, "Relation of Judiciary to the Constitution," *Am. Law Rev.*, XIX, 175 (March–April, 1885); W. M. Meigs, "Some Recent Attacks on the American Doctrine of Judicial Power," *Am. Law Rev.*, XL, 641; A. McF. Davis, "Case of *Frost* vs. *Leighton*," *Am. Hist. Rev.*, II, 229 (1897); E. S. Corwin, "Supreme Court and Unconstitutional Acts of Congress," *Mich. Law Rev.*, June, 1906; E. S. Corwin, "The Establishment of Judicial Review," *Mich. Law Rev.*, X (1910–1911); Professor Trickett, "The Great Usurpation," *Am. Law Rev.*, XL, 396, (May–June, 1906); Justice Gibson in *Eakin* vs. *Raub*, 12 Serg. and Rawle, 330.

the formulated constitutional principle. He wishes to know the real origins of an institution which, though not entirely unique, is nevertheless fundamental and characteristic of the American system.

Perhaps it is not necessary to emphasize the fact that in theory the Supreme Court of the United States is not a special tribunal set up to declare a law of Congress valid or invalid, or established to act as a sort of external censor upon political action. At least if the court occupies any such position now, such was not its original position in the theory of the Constitution or in the mind of the judges of the early days. In theory, any court may exercise the power of holding acts invalid; in doing so it assumes no special and peculiar rôle; for the duty of a court is to declare what the law is and to apply it, and, on the other hand, not to recognize and apply what is not the law; if a legislative act is beyond legislative competence it cannot be law.

Although everyone may readily admit that this is a true theory, common popular opinion does not appear to comprehend the theory, for the statement is commonly made that the courts usurped the right to *control* legislation. It is sometimes said we now have a government by courts. Indeed, in a large part of the discussions of this subject, even by trained scholars, there is a tendency to speak of judicial control over legislation and even to speak of the Supreme Court, as if the question at issue were whether that particular court was established to exercise the power of controlling Congress.

Though, as I have said, my purpose is not to defend the courts in the exercise of this power, or to assert that they have assumed and usurped authority, it is necessary to make it plain that the courts at the beginning did not assume right of control. My question is, therefore, How did it happen that courts in America began, in the latter part of the eighteenth century, to refuse to recognize as law legislative acts which had the appearance of law and which were issued with all the formalities of law? I shall begin with the case of *Marbury* vs. *Madison*, decided in 1803, and, after presenting briefly the position of the Supreme Court of the United States, go backward historically, attempting to discover the foundations or the preparation for this decision.

Marbury vs. *Madison* (1803)

In this case the Supreme Court of the United States for the first time declared a law of

Congress unconstitutional.[1] The facts of the case are familiar. Marbury, who had been appointed by President Adams to a position as justice of the peace in the District of Columbia, had not received his commission, though his appointment had been confirmed by the Senate and his commission had been signed and sealed. Marbury asked the Supreme Court to issue a mandamus to Madison, the Secretary of State, directing Madison to turn over the commission. The Judiciary Act of 1789 had authorized the Supreme Court "to issue writs of mandamus in cases warranted by the principles and usage of law, to any courts appointed, or persons holding office, under the authority of the United States." The court decided that it could not issue this writ of mandamus in an original proceeding and that this portion of the Act of 1789 was unconstitutional. In giving his opinion on this matter, Marshall, referring to the distinction between governments which are limited and those unlimited, said the distinction was abolished if the limits did not confine the persons on whom they were imposed, and if acts prohibited and acts allowed were of equal obligation. "Between these alternatives, there is no middle ground. The Constitution is either a

[1] 1 Cranch 137.

superior paramount law, unchangeable by ordinary means, or it is on a level with ordinary legislative acts, and, like other acts, is alterable when the legislature shall please to alter it. . . . . Certainly, all those who have framed written constitutions contemplated them as forming the fundamental and paramount law of the nation, and consequently, the theory of every such government must be, that an act of the legislature, repugnant to the Constitution, is void.

"This theory is essentially attached to a written constitution, and is, consequently, to be considered by this court as one of the fundamental principles of our society. . . . . It is, emphatically, the province and duty of the Judicial Department to say what the law is. . . . . If two laws conflict with each other, the courts must decide on the operation of each."

Marshall's argument on this phase of the case was brief and direct. To him the Constitution was law, and law meant that the courts were under obligation to accept it and apply it. But of course the mere fact that there was a written constitution in America did not necessarily imply as a logical fact the right of the court to apply that Constitution and ignore the interpretation of the Constitution by the legislative authority; that the Constitution was a law in the sense that it could be and must be maintained by the courts, even when Congress in exercising its legislative power had itself interpreted the Constitution, was the very point at issue. The thing then to be explained is why Marshall assumed that if the Constitution was law, the courts must place their interpretation on it and not recognize the right of the legislative body to determine its own rights under it. The explanation of Marshall's position must be sought in the historical background, not in mere logical disquisition on the Constitution alone;[1] certainly we cannot rest the judicial authority simply on the supposition that a written constitution can and must be interpreted in courts.

IMMEDIATE ANTECEDENTS OF *Marbury* VS. *Madison*, 1789–1803

The Marbury case, as I have already said, was the first decided by the federal Supreme Court in which a congressional act was distinctly declared unconstitutional. There are, however, certain expressions of opinion and dicta by

[1] Of course other states of the world have written constitutions; but they have not as a rule been considered law in the sense that the courts can and must pass on them in opposition to the legislative judgment.

federal judges, and at least some important decisions, which need to be taken into consideration as a preparation for Marshall's decision. In 1798 arose the case of *Calder* vs. *Bull*.[1] This was not a case involving the right of the court to declare a law of Congress unconstitutional; but it was of importance inasmuch as the Supreme Court discussed the validity of state legislation and, in course of the discussion, the judges freely expressed opinion concerning the general scope of judicial powers. Justice Chase declared that an act contrary to the first principles of justice would be void, even without direct constitutional prohibition. Justice Iredell thought that the mere principle of natural right or of fundamental justice[2] could not be considered distinct limitations on legislative competence, but he expressed the decided opinion that acts beyond legislative authority bestowed by the Constitution were void and that in clear cases the courts would so hold.

It may be worthy of notice here that this case

[1] 3 Dallas 386.

[2] At an earlier day he appears to have thought natural justice a limitation. "Without an express constitution the power of the legislature would undoubtedly have been absolute (as the Parliament in Great Britain is held to be), and any act passed, *not inconsistent with natural justice* (for that curb is avowed by the judges even in England), would have been binding on the people."—McRee, *Life of Iredell*, II, 172. See *post*, p. 74, note.

may have been of some influence in the development of the principle we are looking for, because of the intimate logical and practical connection between the right of a federal court to declare a state law invalid, as a violation of the Constitution or law of the United States, and the right to declare a law of Congress invalid. Could a federal court declare a state law unconstitutional and declare a congressional law of precisely similar character constitutional, if both the state legislature and Congress were prohibited by the Constitution from passing such a law? It happens in this case that one matter in question was whether a law was *ex post facto;* and both the United States and the state are forbidden by the Constitution of the United States to pass an *ex post facto* law.

In 1796 arose the case of *Hylton* vs. *the United States,*[1] in which the subject under discussion was the validity of an act providing for a direct tax on carriages. The act was attacked as unconstitutional on the ground that the tax was direct and should have been apportioned among the states. The law was not held invalid, but the reason for bringing the suit was the assumption that the court had the power to declare the act invalid and the arguments before

[1] 3 Dallas 171.

the court are based on that supposition.[1] The case of *Vanhorne's Lessee* vs. *Dorrance*, 1795 (2 Dallas 304), was in the technical sense not strictly a precedent, but it probably prepared the way for the frank exercise of the power in *Marbury* vs. *Madison*. In the Vanhorne case a state statute was declared invalid because contrary to a treaty of the United States. In the course of the opinion Justice Paterson, with considerable fulness, outlined the American system and presented the basis for the exercise of judicial power.[2]

[1] The case of *Ware* vs. *Hylton* (3 Dallas 199) might perhaps be mentioned because in it the court declared in favor of the force of a treaty over state law. This of course is not a direct precedent, but an instance, plainly provided for by the Constitution, of judicial authority in an important matter where state legislation was involved.

[2] *Vanhorne's Lessee* vs. *Dorrance* (2 Dallas 304):

After commenting upon Coke and the statement of Blackstone on the omnipotence of Parliament, Justice Paterson says that "It is difficult to say, what the constitution of England is; because, not being reduced to written certainty and precision, it lies entirely at the mercy of the Parliament: it bends to every governmental exigency; it varies and is blown about by every breeze of legislative humor or political caprice. Some of the judges in England have had the boldness to assert, that an act of Parliament, made against natural equity, is void; but this opinion contravenes the general position, that the validity of an act of Parliament cannot be drawn into question by the judicial department: it cannot be disputed, and must be obeyed. The power of Parliament is absolute and transcendent; it is omnipotent in the scale of political existence. Besides, in England, there is no

Of more importance is the decision of the judges on the circuit in the "First Hayburn case," a distinct declaration, it would seem, of the unconstitutionality of a portion of the act requiring judges to act as pension

written constitution, no fundamental law, nothing visible, nothing real, nothing certain, by which a statute can be tested. In America, the case is widely different: every state in the Union has its constitution reduced to written exactitude and precision.

"What is a constitution? It is the form of government, delineated by the mighty hand of the people, in which certain first principles of fundamental laws are established. The constitution is certain and fixed; it contains the permanent will of the people, and is the supreme law of the land; it is paramount to the power of the legislature, and can be revoked or altered only by the authority that made it. The life-giving principle and the death-doing stroke must proceed from the same hand. What are legislatures? Creatures of the constitution: they owe their existence to the constitution: they derive their powers from the constitution; it is their commission; and therefore, all their acts must be conformable to it, or else they will be void. The constitution is the work or will of the people themselves, in their original, sovereign, and unlimited capacity. Law is the work or will of the legislature, in their derivative and subordinate capacity. The one is the work of the creator, and the other of the creature. The constitution fixes limits to the exercise of legislative authority, and prescribes the orbit within which it must move. In short, gentlemen, the constitution is the sun of the political system, around which all legislative, executive, and judicial bodies must revolve. Whatever may be the case in other countries, yet, in this, there can be no doubt, that every act of the legislature, repugnant to the constitution, is absolutely void.

". . . . The constitution of a state is stable and permanent, not to be worked upon by the temper of the times, nor to rise and fall with the tide of events: notwithstanding the competition of opposing interests, and the violence of contending parties, it remains firm and immovable, as a mountain amidst the strife of

commissioners.[1] Of significance too is the determination of the judges not to act in a judicial capacity or as judges in the performance of their duties as commissioners, a determination made known by them in what is commonly called "the Hayburn case," and reported in a note in 2 Dallas 406.

In the foregoing paragraphs I have mentioned the federal cases and the dicta of the judges which may have served as a preparation for the opinion in *Marbury* vs. *Madison*.[2] Justice

storms, or a rock in the ocean amidst the raging of the waves. I take it to be a clear position: that if a legislative act oppugns a constitutional principle, the former must give way, and be rejected on the score of repugnance. I hold it to be a position equally clear and sound, that, in such case, it will be the duty of the court to adhere to the constitution, and to declare the act null and void. The constitution is the basis of legislative authority; it lies at the foundation of all law, and is a rule and commission by which both legislators and judges are to proceed. It is an important principle, which, in the discussion of questions of the present kind, ought never to be lost sight of, that the judiciary in this country is not a subordinate, but co-ordinate, branch of the government."

[1] See M. Farrand, "The First Hayburn Case," *Am. Hist. Rev.* XIII, 281. Professor Farrand seems to demonstrate that Wilson, Blair, and Peters actually met the issue and declared the law unconstitutional. Reference might also be made to the case *U.S.* vs. *Yale Todd* (1794), referred to in a note in *U.S.* vs. *Ferreira* (13 Howard 52); the case grew out of the pension act referred to above but was not probably a distinct declaration that an act was unconstitutional. See Farrand, *op. cit.*

[2] In December, 1802, Marshall on the circuit in North Carolina (*Ogden* vs. *Witherspoon*, Federal Cases No. 10,461 and 3 N.C. 404), sitting with a federal district judge pronounced an act

Marshall's opinion in the case is sometimes considered brief and summary as well as inconclusive; we ought to bear in mind, however, that the judges in previous opinions had, with considerable clearness and explicitness, stated the principle on which the court acted.

It is not necessary here to consider in detail various remarks made in Congress or in other places that would tend to show the acceptance of the notion that courts had the authority in question or, on the other hand, objections to the principle. It is worth while to notice in passing, however, the opinion of the states in their answer to the Virginia and Kentucky Resolutions where they speak of the Supreme Court of the United States as the final inter-

of the state legislature void because the legislature had assumed judicial authority and violated the principle of separation of the powers. Marshall also believed the state act violated the federal Constitution by impairing the obligations of a contract.

In the case of *Minge* vs. *Gilmour* (1798), Federal Cases No. 9,631, Judge Iredell in the Circuit Court in North Carolina stated the doctrine clearly, but refused to declare the act in question—a state act—void; he expressed his belief, as he did in *Calder* vs. *Bull*, that an act ought not to be held void because contrary to natural justice, though some respectable authorities maintained the right of the courts to take that position. He declined to go farther than asserting that an act contrary to the Constitution is void. Reference should perhaps also be made to Judge Chase's words in *U.S.* vs. *Callender*, Federal Cases No. 14,709. I believe the instances I have given above and in this note cover all the cases and opinions.

preter of the Constitution. And attention should probably here be called to the lectures of James Wilson, one of the most active, able, and influential men in the Philadelphia Convention and one of the judges in the first Hayburn case. In these lectures delivered in 1791 and 1792 to the students of the University of Pennsylvania and a general audience, Wilson fully developed the doctrine that the court had a right to declare a law unconstitutional.[1]

The right of a federal court to declare an act of Congress unconstitutional was not directly and explicitly provided for in the Judiciary Act of 1789. That act is, however, properly considered as a contemporaneous interpretation of the Constitution by men, some of whom were members of the Philadelphia Convention; and it may rightly be used as an indication of how some of the framers of the Constitution looked upon this matter, and also as a part of the background of the Marbury decision and for the position announced in the dicta of the judges in the cases to which I have already called

[1] Wilson's lectures are the more significant from the fact that he coupled his assertion of this power of the court with a statement of the binding effect of divine law and thus, as we shall see more clearly in a later portion of this paper, helped to mark out for us the transition between the older and the later theories of fundamental unchanging law.

attention. Oliver Ellsworth, one of the leading men of the Convention, was the chief advocate of the act when it was before Congress, and to him is commonly attributed chief influence in forming the measure. That act provided for appeal, from the highest state court in which a decision of the suit could be made, to the Supreme Court of the United States, if the state court in passing on the validity of a congressional enactment declared such enactment invalid. This plainly indicates that the Supreme Court of the United States might agree with the state court and thus might co-operate with the state court in refusing to recognize the validity of congressional legislation. It appears therefore as if the passage of this act must be considered as a logical preparation for the independent right of the federal court to deny the validity of congressional enactments.

The argument of Hamilton in the *Federalist* also deserves mention. His discussion of judicial power is extended and explicit. He takes issue with those who have fallen into "perplexity respecting the rights of the courts to pronounce legislative acts void because contrary to the Constitution, from an imagination that the doctrine would imply a superiority of the

Judiciary to the Legislative power." He also calls attention to the position already assumed by the state courts: "The benefits of the integrity and moderation of the Judiciary have already been felt in more States than one; and though they may have displeased those whose sinister expectations they may have disappointed, they must have commanded the esteem and applause of all the virtuous and disinterested."[1]

It is not my intention to present at length the statements made in the state conventions adopting the federal Constitution (1787–1788). In some of the conventions this power of the courts was referred to—by Marshall in Virginia, by Martin in Maryland, by Ellsworth in Connecticut, by Wilson in Pennsylvania. These facts are not complete proof that the men of the enacting conventions intended consciously to bestow the power on the courts; so far as the discussion goes, however, it appears to support the contention that it was supposed that the courts would possess the power.

THE STATE COURTS, 1787–1803

The state judges in the period under consideration had at various times given opinions

[1] *Federalist*, No. LXXVIII.

or expressed sentiments in favor of the general right of a court to declare a law contrary to the Constitution void. Of course I am speaking of state laws and of state constitutions. In *Whittington* vs. *Polk,*[1] a Maryland case, Chief

[1] *Whittington* vs. *Polk,* 1 Harris and Johnson (April, 1802), (Maryland) 236, 241 (the volume does not appear to have been published before 1821):

"Chase, Ch. J.—In the discussion of this case the following points were raised and contended for by the counsel of the plaintiff. 1st, That an act of assembly repugnant to the Constitution is void. 2d, That the courts have a right to determine an act of assembly void, which is repugnant to the Constitution. . . . .

"The *two first points* were conceded by the counsel for the defendant; indeed they have not been controverted in any of the cases which have been brought before this court.

"Notwithstanding these concessions, the court deem it necessary to communicate the reasons and grounds of their opinion on those points.

"The bill of rights and form of government compose the constitution of Maryland, and is a compact made by the people of Maryland among themselves, through the agency of a convention selected and appointed for that important purpose.

"This compact is founded on the principle that the people being the source of power, all government of right originates from them.

"In this compact the people have distributed the powers of government in such manner as they thought would best conduce to the promotion of the general happiness; and for the attainment of that all-important object have, among other provisions, judiciously deposited the legislative, judicial, and executive, in separate and distinct hands, subjecting the functionaries of these powers to such limitations and restrictions as they thought fit to prescribe.

"The legislature, being the creature of the constitution, and acting within a circumscribed sphere, is not omnipotent, and can-

Justice Chase of that state said: "In the decision of the case the following points were raised and contended for by the counsel for the plaintiff: 1st, That an act of assembly repugnant to the Constitution is void; 2d, That the court has a right to determine an act of assembly void, which is repugnant to the

not rightfully exercise any power, but that which is derived from that instrument.

"The constitution having set certain limits or landmarks to the power of the legislature, whenever they exceed them they act without authority, and such acts are mere nullities, not being done in pursuance of power delegated to them: Hence the necessity of some power under the constitution to restrict the acts of the legislature within the limits defined by the constitution.

"The power of determining finally on the validity of the acts of the legislature cannot reside with the legislature, because such power would defeat and render nugatory, all the limitations and restrictions on the authority of the legislature, contained in the bill of rights and form of government, and they would become judges of the validity of their own acts, which would establish a despotism, and subvert that great principle of the constitution, which declares that the powers of making, judging, and executing the law, shall be separate and distinct from each other.

"This power cannot be exercised by the people at large, or in their collective capacity, because they cannot interfere according to their own compact, unless by elections, and in such manner as the constitution has prescribed, and because there is no other mode ascertained by which they can express their will.

[Two paragraphs giving reason why ordinary political remedies and elections are not sufficient.]

". . . . It is the office and province of the court to decide all questions of law which are judicially brought before them, according to the established mode of proceeding, and to determine whether an act of the legislature, which assumes the appearance

Constitution. . . . . [Two other points are given.] The two first points were conceded by the counsel for the defendant; indeed they have not been controverted in any of the cases which have been brought before this court." The judge goes on, however, to develop the basis of this power. In this case, the court did not declare a law invalid, but it announced its authority to do so. We should notice that the

of a law, and is clothed with the garb of authority, is made pursuant to the power vested by the constitution in the legislature; for if it is not the result or emanation of authority derived from the constitution, it is not law, and cannot influence the judgment of the court in the decision of the question before them.

"The oath of a judge is 'that he will do equal right and justice according *to the law of this state*, in every case in which he shall act as judge.'

"To do right and justice according to the law, the judge must determine what the law is, which necessarily involves in it the right of examining the constitution (which is the supreme or paramount law, and under which the legislature derive the only authority they are invested with, of making laws), and considering whether the act passed is made pursuant to the constitution, and that trust and authority which is delegated thereby to the legislative body.

"The three great powers or departments of government are independent of each other, and the legislature, as such, can claim no superiority or pre-eminence over the other two. The legislature are the trustees of the people, and, as such, can only move within those lines which the constitution has defined as the boundaries of their authority, and if they should incautiously, or unadvisedly transcend those limits, the constitution has placed the judiciary as the barrier or safeguard to resist the oppression, and redress the injuries which might accrue from such inadvertent, or unintentional infringements of the constitution."

court distinctly put forth the facts of the separation of the powers of government.

In 1796 in the matter of Lindsay and others against the Commissioner,[1] a South Carolina case, there was a difference of opinion. Judge

[1] *Lindsay and others* vs. *the Commissioner*, 1796; 2 Bay (S.C.) 38, 61 (the book was printed in 1811):

"He said, it was painful to him to be obliged to question the exercise of any legislative power, but he was sworn to support the constitution, and this was the most important of all the duties which were incumbent on the judges. On the faithful performance of this high duty would depend the integrity and duration of our government. If the legislature is permitted to exercise other rules than those ordained by the constitution, and if innovations are suffered to acquire the sanction of time and practice, the rights of the people will soon become dependent on legislative will, and the constitution have no more obligation than an obsolete law. But if this court does its duty, in giving to the constitution an overruling operation over every act of the legislature which is inconsistent with it, the people will then have an independent security for their rights, which may render them perpetual. In exercising this high authority, the judges claim no judicial supremacy; they are only the administrators of the public will. If an act of the legislature is held void, it is not because the judges have any control over the legislative power, but because the act is forbidden by the constitution, and because the will of the people, which is therein declared, is paramount to that of their representatives, expressed in any law. As the act under consideration appeared to him to be repugnant to this high will, he was bound to say, that it ought not to have any operation, and that the prohibition should be granted."

This was the opinion of Judge Waties, who appears to have been in accord with Judge Burke.

The judges were equally divided in the case and the applicants took nothing by their motion. There was no doubt that the validity of the law came distinctly before the court and the judges were divided on the subject.

Waties, supported by Judge Burke, asserted this right and said "if an act of the legislature is held void, it is not because the judges have any control over the legislative power, but because the act is forbidden by the constitution, and because the will of the people, which is therein declared, is paramount to that of their representatives expressed in any law." In 1794 the judges of North Carolina appear to have been in conflict, although the basis on which the judges acted in holding the law not void is not clear. Judge Williams, while sitting alone, declared the act in question unconstitutional, but two other judges a few days later proceeded on the principle that the act of the legislature was good.[1]

[1] Haywood's Reports (N.C.), I, 28, 29, 40. *State* vs. ———:

"At the last session of the General Assembly, it was enacted that judgments might be obtained by the Attorney-General against receivers of public money, by motion; and that their delinquencies should be sufficient notice to them that they were to be proceeded against: and upon this act the Attorney-General now moved for judgment against several, and produced the act to shew how he was authorized so to do.

"But Judge Williams stopped him, saying he could not permit judgments to be taken in that manner. That he conceived the act to be unconstitutional, it was to condemn a man unheard. The 12th article of the Bill of Rights says, 'No freeman ought to be taken, imprisoned or disseised of his freehold, liberties or property, &c. but by the law of the land'; and these words mean, according to the course of the common law; which always required the party to be cited, and to have a day in court upon which he might appear and defend himself. The 14th section declares,

The court of South Carolina in the case of *Bowman and others* (1792), *devisees of Cattell* vs. *Middleton*, declared a law of 1712 "*ipso facto*

that the ancient mode of trial by jury, is one of the best securities of the rights of the people, and ought to remain sacred and inviolable. The ancient mode of trial by jury was, that after the defendant was cited, and had pleaded, and the other party had denied his plea, or some part of it, then the point in controversy was submitted to the decision of a jury; but here, though a jury may be sworn, what will it be upon? It will be upon a default taken against the party who does not appear and plead, because he has no knowledge that any proceedings are intended to be had against him; and so in truth it is not a trial by jury according to the ancient mode—the defendant has no opportunity of making any defensive allegations which may be submitted to the decision of a jury; but the jury here are merely to pronounce what is the sum to be recovered, and in this they are to be governed by the report of the comptroller, which is made evidence against the defendant by another act of Assembly; so that in reality the jury have nothing to determine on—it is mere form for the sake of which they are to be impanneled—such a trial is a mere farce. I think the act unconstitutional, and I cannot, as at present advised, give my assent to its being carried into effect—the Judges of the land are a branch of the government, and are to administer the constitutional laws, not such as are repugnant to the constitution; it is their duty to resist an unconstitutional act. In fact, such an act made by the General Assembly, who are deputed only to make laws in conformity to the constitution, and within the limits it prescribes, is not any law at all. Whenever the Assembly exceeds the limits of the constitution, they act without authority, and then their acts are no more binding than the acts of any other assembled body. . . . .

"Judge Williams still adhered to his opinion of yesterday, giving nearly the same reasons he then gave.

"At Halifax court a few days after, the Attorney-General again moved the court, consisting of Judge Ashe and Judge Macay, and stated to them the arguments which had been used at Hillsborough: after hearing him, the court took time to advise for a

void" because it was against common right as well as against Magna Charta.[1] In 1793 in the case of *Kamper* vs. *Hawkins*[2] the Virginia court

few days; when the matter being moved again, Judge Ashe gave the opinion of the court, saying he and Judge Macay had conferred together—that for himself he had had very considerable doubts, but that Judge Macay was very clear in his opinion that the judgments might be taken, and had given such strong reasons, that his (Judge Ashe's) objections were vanquished, and therefore that the Attorney-General might proceed—but that yet he did not very well like it.—So the judgments were taken."

[1] 1 Bay (S.C.) 252, 254 (the volume appears to have been published in 1809):

"The question was of the validity of an act passed in 1712 transferring the freehold from the heir at law, one Nicholls, and also from the eldest son and heir of John Cattell, deceased, investing it in the second son, William Cattell, without a trial by jury; considered null and void.

"*The Court* (present, Grimke and Bay, Justices), who, after a full consideration on the subject, were clearly of opinion, that the plaintiffs could claim no title under the act in question, as it was against common right, as well as against *magna charta*, to take away the freehold of one man and vest it in another, and that, too, to the prejudice of third persons, without any compensation, or even a trial by the jury of the country, to determine the right in question. That the act was, therefore, *ipso facto* void. That no length of time could give it validity, being originally founded on erroneous principles. That the parties, however, might, if they chose, rely upon a possessory right, if they could establish it."

[2] 1 Virginia Cases 20. In *Stidger* vs. *Rogers* (1801), 2 Kentucky 52, an act was declared unconstitutional. In *State* vs. *Parkhurst* (1802), 4 Halstead, N.J. 427, the court laid down the doctrine distinctly, stated the facts and the decision of *Holmes* vs. *Walton* (see *post*, p. 41), and mentioned another case, *Taylor* vs. *Reading*, which I have not been able to find in the New Jersey reports, in which a law was held void. *Austin* vs. *Trustees*

decided that an act contrary to the constitution could not be executed, and after long and thorough discussion of the principles refused to execute the act in question. Two of the judges referred to Vattel, one of them quoting at length a passage from Vattel's *Law of Nature and of Nations*, to which reference is made in later pages of this paper.

The Virginia Court of Appeals in 1792, in the case of *Turner* vs. *Turner's Executrix*,[1] did not declare a law unconstitutional; but in giving prospective rather than retrospective application to the law, the court said: "It is the business of legislators to make the laws; and of the judges to expound them. Having made the law, the legislature have no authority afterward to explain its operation upon things already done under it. They may amend as to future cases, but they cannot prescribe a rule of construction, as to the past." The reason given was declared to be the same as

(1793), 1 Yeates, Penn. 260, is not a distinct precedent, but the judges evidently considered that the court had the power. In *Respublica* vs. *Duquet* (1799), 2 Yeates 493, the court says a law will not be pronounced unconstitutional save in a clear case. The principle is laid down in *Commonwealth* vs. *Franklin*, a Pennsylvania case reported in *Am. Law Jour.*, II, new series, 287.

[1] 4 Call 234, 237. At the very least an interesting example of the way in which the courts will use fundamental law to control and mould legislative enactment.

that which was operated against *ex post facto* laws.

The "Case of the Judges"[1] in Virginia, in 1788–1789, was doubtless well known and was of importance because the court explained at considerable length the relation of the judicial and legislative branches of the government, the independence of the judiciary, and the basis of its power to refuse recognition of an act transcending the constitution. The issues involved were complicated and need not be here given in detail. The court denied the right of the legislature, by an act establishing district courts, to add to the duties and burdens of the judges of the High Court of Appeals, declaring that the additional onerous burdens without additional compensation constituted an attack upon the independence of the judiciary. The judges refused to "do anything officially in execution of an act which appeared to be contrary to the spirit of the constitution." In a remonstrance to the General Assembly, they say, "To obviate a possible objection, that the court, while they are maintaining the independence of the judiciary, are countenancing encroachments of that branch upon the department of others, and assuming a right to control

[1] 4 Call 135.

the legislature, it may be observed that when they decide between an act of the people, and an act of the legislature, they are within the line of their duty, declaring what the law is, and not making a new law." The legislature altered the law but on the same day passed another, reconstituting the Court of Appeals. To this act the judges again objected, contending that an act of the Assembly could not deprive judges of their offices; but because of their general sympathy with the purposes of the act, they resigned and the new system went into effect.

A consideration of all the cases I have mentioned, and all the dicta and opinions of the judges, discloses that the belief was evidently held by the judges, in the early years after the Constitution of the United States was adopted, that courts in general and because of the nature of our constitutions possessed this power and were under obligations to exercise it. Courts from one end of the land to the other assumed this power, and acted on the same principle. The judges were, it seems, not acting strictly on precedent. Indeed, the striking fact is that they commonly did not refer to precedents; but they thought *alike* and along *similar* lines. Cases were at that time not immediately printed and put within reach of judges and lawyers. A number of the books of reports referred to in this paper were not printed till long after the decision. It is a curious fact that in a case decided in the U.S. District Court in Massachusetts in 1808, although the court brings together such opinions and decisions as it can, even *Marbury* vs. *Madison*(!) was unknown to the judge until after his decision was announced; it was referred to in an added footnote to the case.[1]

THE CONSTITUTION AND THE CONSTITUTIONAL CONVENTION OF 1787

The question may now be asked, Why this search for precedents and for expressions of opinion on this subject in the years following the federal Convention? Why not turn to the Constitution and to the Convention at once and discover there the power claimed by the court? The answer is of course that the Constitution is not explicit and that the Convention's debates do not, beyond all possibility of cavil or doubt, solve the question concerning the power of the court. Let us first examine the Constitution.

Mr. Brinton Coxe, in his able book on the *Judicial Power and Unconstitutional Legislation*,

[1] See *Am. Law Jour.* (old series), II (1809), 255, 264.

maintains that the Constitution provides for such a power in the courts because it declares that the Constitution shall be the supreme law of the land and because, in giving the extent of judicial authority, it says that such authority shall extend to controversies arising under the Constitution. Though the Constitution by these phrases necessarily implies the interpretation of the Constitution, to contend that they were beyond question consciously intended to give the courts power to pass on the validity of congressional acts is going too far; for judicial interpretation of the Constitution might well be necessitated without the necessity of considering the validity of congressional enactments, and even where no congressional law was under consideration. That portion of the Constitution therefore which describes the extent of judicial authority may justly be omitted from special discussion.

The clause declaring that the Constitution, laws, and treaties are the supreme law of the land certainly, however, deserves attention. The Constitution is made law, and laws are to be enforced in courts. The very fact that the Constitution is a law, and is so solemnly declared, is of much moment in any consideration of this matter. But this particular clause goes on to say that "the judges in every state shall be bound thereby, anything in the Constitution or laws of the respective states to the contrary notwithstanding." This means that the state judges shall obey and apply the Constitution of the United States as law, even as against their state constitutions and statutes. But does it mean that the courts shall also refuse to recognize as valid a federal law which they consider beyond the power of Congress? It must be said that the framers of the Constitution, when they framed this particular clause, had, probably, uppermost in their minds the great danger of the time, the tendency of the states to act in disregard of their duties and obligations under the articles of union. It appears, however, as I have already said, of immense moment that the Constitution should be called *law*, and if we take into consideration the probable intention, made more evident by the Judiciary Act of 1789, to give the federal Supreme Court the right to decide whether the state courts had recognized the binding effect of the Constitution, we strengthen the reasonable presumption, that, when the Constitution was declared law, the lawyers and logicians of the Convention, men like Wilson and Ellsworth, would inevitably suppose that the Constitution was in general to be enforced in the courts, even when an act of Congress was opposed to it.

It appears strange that those who assert that the courts of the United States usurped power do not recognize, in their view of the background or in their assertions that there was no constitutional provision authorizing such judicial action, this fact of supreme importance. At least by plain constitutional provision state courts are called upon to declare state enactments violating the Constitution, laws, and treaties to be invalid. And thus is clearly recognized the use of *courts* for such purpose. I am not now arguing that this clause in the Constitution is a direct mandate to federal courts to declare a law of Congress unconstitutional. But I am arguing that the mandate to the state courts clearly establishes a notion of the Constitution as law enforceable in the courts; and the inclusion of this provision in the Constitution certainly serves as a psychological background; it shows that the framers of the Constitution had clearly reached a state of mind in which they were ready to declare that state courts should act independently of legislative authority in the state and apply superior law. The very presence of such a provision in the Constitution proves that the framers had at the very least passed some distance from the position, which we are sometimes assured is the only reasonable one, namely the obligation of courts to recognize legislative acts as valid. In one most important particular the framers called upon *courts* to act, and recognized their independence and peculiar power; and it is this conception, this general appreciation of the power and place of courts, which needs special explanation. Nothing in fact is more momentous than the conception of the Constitution as law—a constitution, which outlined and determined relationships between governments and fixed the principles of federal order in a composite state, was to be applied like ordinary law in a court. This is of supreme importance, even if the framers had consciously in mind only the function of state courts in passing upon the validity of state action under the Constitution of the United States. All other provisions of the Constitution bearing on courts and judicial authority and all omissions of distinct statement are unimportant as compared with the fact, that the fundamental law which established federalism was for judicial cognizance and enforcement.

Anyone desiring to understand the importance of the courts and the place they have come to occupy in our constitutional system, as men viewed the situation of those days, would have to understand the tendencies which prompted men to turn to courts and the judicial enforcement of law as of basic significance in any scheme of constitutional order.[1] The maintenance of the treaties of the Confederation, as over against state enactments violating the treaties, had been brought into discussion, and the duty of the courts to abide by the legislation of Congress had been considered in the days before the Convention of 1787 met.

Just how this principle developed it is very difficult to say. Possibly no distinct presentation of it appeared earlier than the act of Congress of the Confederation, April 13, 1787, declaring that states cannot rightly pass any act or acts interpreting, limiting, or impeding the operation of a national treaty, and that when treaties are "constitutionally made" they

[1] I am dwelling upon this aspect of the case because the constant inquiry is, Why should courts dare to exercise such an important function as to declare legislative acts invalid? Such presumption on the part of the courts is, I maintain, more easily understood if we realize that legislators and constitution-makers had already turned to state courts as great instrumentalities for the defense and maintenance of constitutional order. I have in mind, when I speak of constitutional order, the order in the federal or composite system; the courts were called upon to disregard state legislative acts, in order that national authority or federal order might be preserved.

become a "part of the law of the land." The act also called on the legislatures to repeal the acts in general terms and to authorize the courts to decide cases in accordance with the treaty, rather than in accordance with a state law at variance with a treaty. Probably back of this resolution was, in some degree, the force of experience in the old colonial system of Great Britain, of which something will be said later on in this paper. However this may be, the contention or the belief that state acts, contravening treaties or acts of Congress under the Confederation, might be or ought to be considered void, must be connected with the development of the principle that state courts should hold them void,[1] and this prepared the way for the announcement in the Constitution that constitutional laws and treaties are the supreme law of the land.

It is unnecessary here to enter upon a full consideration of the discussion in the federal Convention of 1787. If one confines his attention to such records of debate as we have, he

[1] See Richard Henry Lee to George Mason in Rowland, *Life, Correspondence and Speeches of George Mason*, II, 107; Alexander Hamilton, *Works* (Lodge ed.), I, 288, the third defect—the want of a federal judiciary; Article 19 in Report of the Grand Committee of Congress proposing amendments to the Articles, in Bancroft, *History of the Constitution*, II, 374.

may be left in uncertainty as to whether or not the framers intended to bestow this power upon the courts. They undoubtedly considered the subject, chiefly in connection with the proposition to join the judges with the President in the revision of the laws. In a recent article by Professor Beard there is an attempt in a clever manner, by various tests, to show at least strong presumption that the framers must have supposed the courts would exercise this power. His investigations are of great force, if they are not absolutely conclusive; I shall not attempt here to investigate the discussions of the Convention but only make reference to this article.[1]

[1] "The Supreme Court—Usurper or Grantee," *Political Science Quarterly*, March, 1912, p. 1. Professor Beard's method is to consider not alone what was said in the Convention but what was said by men, especially the leaders, both in the Convention and at other times. There are a few facts which he does not give (and he does not pretend to have made his investigation absolutely exhaustive) which used, in the same manner, strengthen the contention of his article. For example, Brearly, a member of the Convention from New Jersey, had actually, as chief justice of the state, pronounced an act unconstitutional (*Holmes* vs. *Walton*, see below). Paterson, another member, was attorney-general of New Jersey when Brearly gave his decision; and Justice Paterson clearly gave his opinion in *Vanhorne's Lessee* vs. *Dorrance*, mentioned above. Livingston, also a New Jersey member of the Philadelphia Convention, was governor when the case was decided. Gouverneur Morris, in an address to the Pennsylvania legislature in 1785, referred to the New Jersey case and said, "Such power in the judges is dangerous; but unless it somewhere exists, the time employed in framing a bill of rights and form

In making up our minds as to the purpose of the framers of the Constitution, it is necessary to remember that the power of a court to declare a law unconstitutional, as I have already said, does not imply the superiority of the court to the legislative branch of government. And we need not suppose that the men that made the Constitution necessarily believed that a refusal of a court to recognize a law as constitutional meant that the court was set aside as a kind of external tribunal, as a body of censors. Indeed, judging by the various opinions, to some of which I have already referred, it is plain that

of government was merely thrown away." Luther Martin in *Wittington* vs. *Polk* acknowledged that a court could declare an act void; this was some years after the Convention. Brearly again declared a law void in 1797, according to the court in 4 Halstead 444, cited above.

It appears to be supposed sometimes that the framers of the Constitution were unable to agree concerning the problem of judicial authority to declare laws unconstitutional; and it is sometimes intimated that they were uncertain of popular approval or in fear of popular disapproval if they bestowed such power on the courts; in consequence they avoided distinct statements. But there could not well have been much fear of such disapproval by the people if the power were given to declare acts of the national legislature void; the Convention plainly gave the power to state courts to declare invalid not only acts of state legislatures but the state constitutions themselves. The really difficult problem before the Convention was whether or not to establish an inferior federal judiciary. On this subject the Convention took refuge in compromise, or at least in inexplicit statement. On this matter they had reason to feel real concern.

the courts approached this subject from the point of view of their separate independence, rather than because of any duty or responsibility for checking legislative action.

It must be said, however, that the framers of the Constitution, as well as many others of the time, were interested in providing a system of checks and balances whereby one department of the government would restrain the others. The men at Philadelphia were desirous of establishing a strong government capable of protecting property and capable also of protecting liberty and maintaining order. But, though desiring peace and order and government, like other men of the Revolutionary epoch the framers were afraid of government and were quite as desirous of working out a system of restraints as they were of giving efficiency to government. They wished to protect individual right and property. Through these years, therefore, the courts were sometimes considered as constituting a valuable check on legislative or executive action. We find this power of the courts occasionally spoken of as a method of regulating or controlling the conduct of the other branches of government. From what has been already said, however, and from the evidence given later in this paper, we see that the courts did not obtain and exercise this power because men felt that an extraneous superior authority should be established, but because of the separate and independent position in which the courts were established and because of their particular function to declare and apply the law.

PRINCIPLES AND PRECEDENTS, 1776–87

So far in our examination we have traversed some sixteen years, tracing historical facts backward from 1803 to the Constitutional Convention of 1787. But it should be pointed out that, even if we had discovered in the Constitutional Convention a distinct intention to bestow this power on the courts, we should not have satisfied our curiosity as to the source of this principle. The men of 1787 certainly did not create the principle out of their imaginations. It is, therefore, once again necessary to work our way backward to discover the emergence of principles before the meeting of the Convention.

Students who have examined the subject under discussion, the origin of judicial power in this country, have commonly referred to various cases in the state courts, in the period between the outbreak of the Revolution and the meeting of the federal Convention; to this matter we may now turn our attention. I shall not examine these cases, however, strictly as precedents in any technical sense; but consider them as forming an historical background; and I shall have in mind also the method of approach followed by the judges, and the nature or the course of their reasoning. There were in this period a few cases in which state legislative acts were declared unconstitutional by state courts or in which the principle of independent interpretation was announced by the judges in the state courts. These cases and opinions are of considerable importance as more than mere legal precedents in any narrow or technical sense. They disclose the situation and present the state of mind; moreover, it should be noticed that this position was not justified by any declaration in the state constitutions that the constitution was law or, in some cases, by the distinct announcement in the state constitutions that the courts were an independent and separate branch of the government. The first case, a most important one, was that of *Holmes* vs. *Walton*, a New Jersey case decided in 1780, in which a law of the state of New Jersey was declared unconstitutional.[1]

[1] See "*Holmes* vs. *Walton*, the New Jersey Precedent," by Austin Scott in *Am. Hist. Rev.*, IV, 456. It is worthy of note

The second case is the case of *Caton* vs. *Commonwealth of Virginia*, decided in 1782.[1] Judge Wythe in this case said: "I have heard of an English chancellor who said, and it was nobly said, that it was his duty to protect the rights of the subject against the encroachments of the crown; and that he would do it, at every hazard." After speaking of his duty to protect one branch of the legislature, Judge Wythe went on to say, "Nay more, if the whole legislature,

that Brearly, the chief justice who rendered the decision, Paterson, the attorney-general, and Livingston, the governor at the time the decision was rendered, were delegates from New Jersey to the federal Convention. They were interested in the formation of the New Jersey or small state plan, and it was through this plan that the clause declaring the Constitution, laws, and treaties of the United States the law of the land, worked its way into the Constitution of the United States. It will not do to stress the connection between *Holmes* vs. *Walton* and this section of the Constitution; it is possible, but we cannot say more, that the case was of influence on the minds of men like Paterson when the small state men in their plan provided that laws and treaties should be "the supreme law of the respective states" and that the judges of the states should be bound thereby. Paterson was on the supreme bench when *Marbury* vs. *Madison* was decided.

[1] 4 Call (Virginia) 5, 8. The question involved was whether or not a pardon passed by the House of Delegates constituted a constitutional pardon. The court decided that the action of the House without the co-operation of the other branch of the General Assembly was not conclusive. The case was not so simple as it might appear because there was at least some ground for asserting that the power belonged to the House of Delegates. The whole question of the right to declare a law unconstitutional arose in the discussion of the case. There was some question of the general validity of the treason law of 1776.

an event to be deprecated, should attempt to overlap the bounds, prescribed to them by the people, I, in administering the public justice of the country, will meet the united powers, at my seat in this tribunal; and, pointing to the constitution, will say, to them, here is the limit of your authority; and, hither, shall you go, but no further."[1]

The case of *Rutgers* vs. *Waddington* is often cited as an example or precedent. It arose in the Mayor's Court of the City of New York in 1784.[2] The case, however, did not directly declare a law unconstitutional, though the court was accused of having taken that position. What the court did do was to interpret the act and to pass upon the purpose of the legislature in passing it in such a way as to make it inap-

[1] The connection between the right to protect against executive action and the right to protect against legislative action is noteworthy. Judge Blair was a member of the court when this case was decided. He was a member of the Philadelphia Convention and was for a short time a judge in the Supreme Court of the United States. The report says (4 Call 20), "Chancellor Blair and the rest of the judges, were of the opinion that the court had power to declare any resolution or act of the legislature or either branch of it, to be unconstitutional and void." Judge Pendleton was not so sure. Pendleton, however, was a member of the court when the judges took the position in the Case of the Judges previously mentioned.

[2] See Thayer, *Leading Cases*, I, 63. Hamilton, one of the members of the Philadelphia Convention, was one of the attorneys in the case.

plicable to the facts at issue. The court did not distinctly set itself up as paramount to the legislative body or as controlled by a superior law. The court said that judges are not at liberty to reject a law where the intention is manifest. "But when a law is expressed in general words, and some collateral matter, which happens to arise from those general words, is unreasonable, there the judges are in decency to conclude, that the consequences were not foreseen by the legislature; and therefore they are at liberty to expound the statute by equity, and only *quoad hoc* to disregard it."[1] The position of the judges in this matter is of considerable interest in light of what will be said later on in this paper concerning the way in which the courts in England at an earlier day, as well as the courts in this country, felt free to interpret legislative acts in such a way as to make them ineffective while they were pretending not to disregard the statute *in toto*.

In Rhode Island in 1786 arose the well-known case of *Trevett* vs. *Weeden*.[2] It is note-

[1] This statement is practically a quotation from Blackstone, Introd., § 3, par. 20, No. 91.

[2] The best source for understanding this case is a pamphlet by James M. Varnum, the attorney for the defense in the case, printed in Providence in 1787. It appears to be fully reprinted in P. W. Chandler, *Am. Criminal Trials* (1844), II, 269. This

worthy that Rhode Island continued under her old charter. It is true that this may be considered a written constitution, but it was not a written constitution emanating in full from the people like constitutions of the other states, with the exception of that of Connecticut. Moreover there was nothing in the charter or constitution of Rhode Island explicitly providing against the sort of legislative measure which the court was considering in this case. Without attempting to consider the various aspects of the discussion or the basis of the decision at length, I wish to call especial attention to the statement in the argument of James M. Varnum, the attorney for Weeden. He declared the right to jury trial was a fundamental constitutional right, always claimed and ratified as such and always held most dear and sacred; that the legislature derived all its powers from the constitution and had no power of making laws but in subordination of the constitution, and therefore could not violate the constitution by depriving citizens of jury trial; that the

volume at least gives Varnum's speech. A material statement is given in Thayer, *Cases on Constitutional Law*, I, 73; and the argument is in Coxe, *Judicial Power and Unconstitutional Legislation*, 236. Coxe calls attention to the use of Vattel in *Bayard* vs. *Singleton*, but does not seem to know that the Massachusetts legislators had done much to popularize the doctrine. See *post*, p. 70.

act was therefore unconstitutional and so void; that the court had power to judge and determine what acts of the General Assembly were agreeable to the constitution; that the court was under obligations to execute the laws of the land and therefore could not, would not, consider this act as a law of the land. He referred to Locke and Vattel and particularly to that portion of Vattel in which the question is discussed as to whether legislatures have the right to legislate in disregard of the fundamental law; he quoted the argument in which Vattel concludes that the legislature cannot change the constitution without destroying the foundations of its own authority. On the ground that the act was unconstitutional the court refused to take cognizance of the information.

Another valuable precedent is that of *Bayard and Wife* vs. *Singleton*, a North Carolina case decided in 1787.[1] In this case the court clearly declared a law unconstitutional, and the following statement from the court is of special significance: "But that it was clear, that no Act they could pass, could by any means repeal or alter the constitution, because, if they could

[1] 1 Martin (N.C.) 42. The exact title is *Den on the dem. of Bayard and wife* vs. *Singleton*. It is plain that the court had in mind the statement of Vattel, used also by Varnum in the argument in *Trevett* vs. *Weeden*. Judge Ashe called attention to the separation of the powers.

do this, they would at the same instant of time, destroy their own existence as a Legislature, and dissolve the government thereby established. Consequently the constitution (which the judicial power was bound to take notice of as much as of any other law whatever), standing in full force as the fundamental law of the land, notwithstanding the act on which the present motion was grounded, the same act must of course, in that instance, stand as abrogated and without any effect."

It is sometimes said that there was a Massachusetts case not far from this time. J. B. Cutting wrote to Jefferson commenting upon the recent proceeding of the Virginia Court of Appeals, evidently referring to the Case of the Judges which I have mentioned above. He also said that an act of the legislature was declared unconstitutional by the Supreme Court of Massachusetts, and at the next session of the legislature the law was repealed, although he doubted the necessity of such a procedure.[1]

According to Judge Tucker, a case arose in

[1] Bancroft, *History of the Constitution*, II, 472, 473; A. C. Goodell, Jr., "An Early Constitutional Case in Massachusetts," *Harvard Law Review*, VII. Mr. Goodell is of the opinion that this case was one in which the court of the state refused to hold valid an act passed on the subject of British debts by the Massachusetts legislature, an act contrary to the treaty of peace and encroaching upon the power of Congress under the Articles of Confederation, i.e., the Constitution.

Virginia in 1778 in which the courts refused to abide by an act of the legislature. This is called the case of Josiah Philips. Philips was taken and tried according to the ordinary course of law, in spite of the fact that an act of attainder had been passed by the legislature. Tucker says the court refused to pass the sentence pursuant to the direction of the act. "This is decisive proof of the importance of the separation of the powers of government, and of the independence of the judiciary."[1] The evidence is by no means conclusive that the court declined to recognize the constitutionality of the bill of attainder; it appears probable that the judges intimated their objections to Mr. Randolph, the attorney-general, and that in consequence Philips was regularly tried and convicted. It is not at all impossible, however, that this case may have been later looked upon, despite various distortions of the facts, as a case in which the court asserted its independent right to interpret the constitution.[2]

These precedents, we are told, are not very valuable precedents for courts to act upon. I am citing them, not so much as precedents in

[1] Tucker's *Blackstone*, I, Appendix, 293.

[2] The whole case is illuminatingly discussed by W. P. Trent, "The Case of Josiah Philips," *Am. Hist. Rev.*, I, 444.

the strict legal sense, as an indication of judicial opinion and of the general state of mind toward courts and legislatures. Attention has also been called to the fact that there was a good deal of opposition in the states to the exercise of this authority by the courts. Of this I think there is little doubt, though evidently there were decided differences of opinion. During the whole period of the Confederation there were marked social and political disturbances.[1] Men of substance and of conservative temperament, anxious for the establishment of sound government and permanent institutions, were, as everyone knows, distressed by the situation. There was danger that the legislators representing the extreme popular opinion would disregard fundamental rights of property and of individual liberty; many of the popular politicians were not ready to acquiesce in the political enforcement of fundamental principles of the constitution or of individual right, when such enforcement meant the annulment of measures in which they had particular interest, such as the enforced circulation of worthless

[1] There undoubtedly were objections and criticisms. It should be noticed, however, that Gerry in the federal Convention, on June 4, said: "In some states the judges had actually set aside laws, as being against the Constitution. This was done, too, with general approbation."

paper money in Rhode Island. If this restless, popular element had been the chief force and influence in establishing our institutions or in building and establishing the Constitution of the United States, more importance would need to be assigned to certain evidences of dissatisfaction with judicial determinations; but, as everyone knows, such was not the case. Indeed, it might justly be said that the popular unrest and distrust were elements favoring the authority of the courts and the inviolability of the constitutions, rather than strong influences making for the free power of the legislature and the impotence of the courts. The conditions in North Carolina[1] and Rhode Island, for example, offered strong temptations to the courts to act in support of reasonable justice and order.

SEPARATION OF THE POWERS; REVOLUTIONARY SENTIMENT

We have now succeeded in working our way back some eight or ten years before the meeting of the Philadelphia Convention, and have seen that in a few instances cases were decided or sentiments were expressed in the state courts favorable to the exercise of this judicial author-

[1] The North Carolina situation is in part shown in McRee's *Life of Iredell*, II, ch. xix. The condition is well known.

ity, the origin of which we are considering. It must be said, however, that we have not succeeded in getting back very far; for we must once more inquire how it happened that the state courts ventured to set themselves up as judges of the constitution and to declare acts of state legislatures void and of no effect. In order to account for this we must find antecedent conditions accounting for attitudes of courts toward constitutions and legislative bodies, or accounting for the prevalence of these significant principles. Let us first notice a fact to which I have already called attention,[1] namely that the state courts did not assert that they were peculiarly and particularly set up as guardians of the state constitution or censors of legislative action. They maintained that the state constitution was binding upon the legislature and upon the courts, and that the courts were not under obligations to put into effect an act at variance with the constitution. They asserted this power, not because they were superior to the legislature, but because they were independent. This authority, then, in part arose from the recognition of the separa-

[1] I make no apology for my repetition of this fact; for the failure to realize it has vitiated much able discussion of the subject. If that point is not made clear or is not accepted, there is no use in any prolonged discussion.

tion of the powers of government; from the conviction that the courts were not under the control of a co-ordinate branch of the government, but were entirely able to interpret the constitution themselves when acting within their own field. It is thus apparent that the course which judicial reasoning took was in part determined by this principle of the separation of the powers, a sense of independent authority and of independent responsibility. Someone will say that this assumption of independence is entirely fallacious, that in reality the courts were controlling legislation. However that may be, the courts, as I have just maintained, approached the subject from the point of view of independence and not of superiority.

In this connection it may be well to consider this principle of the separation of powers of government in its origin and its effect. The introduction of this doctrine of the separation of the powers was due in considerable measure, as everyone knows, to the influence of Montesquieu's book on *The Spirit of the Law*, which was often referred to by the men of the later eighteenth century. Montesquieu, as all know, believed he discovered this principle of the separation of the powers in the system of the

English government.[1] It is sometimes said that in this respect he was entirely mistaken, for, in fact, the powers of government were in England peculiarly connected and the legislative branch of the government was possessed of supreme and complete authority. Some aspects of this subject I shall take up more fully later on, only pointing out the fact now that there was considerable truth in Montesquieu's assertion; for the judges, while doubtless in the eighteenth century subject to Parliament, had a position of peculiar authority which they had inherited from earlier times; they exercised authority over all agents of the government instead of being compelled to accept the principle that the executive agents were acting in accordance with direction from a political superior. The principle that the king can do no wrong has for its corollary the principle, more important than the main proposition, that his agents are personally responsible. Even in the latter half of the eighteenth century, the courts, whatever may be said of the theory of English institutions, occupied a position of substantial freedom. They would not or could not, in the eighteenth century, have declared a law of Parliament

[1] It is noteworthy that John Dickinson did too, though he may have been guided by Montesquieu.

void; but, as I have said, their relations toward administrative officers and their general power show that they were in a position of independence, dignity, and influence.

It can hardly be said, however, that the American doctrine of the separation of the powers was entirely absorbed from Montesquieu. While there are some declarations and contentions that point in the direction of legislative superiority, the course of American constitutional development, from 1760[1] or thereabouts, was making for the development of a sentiment in favor of the independence of the departments and the separation of the powers of government. And that principle was thoroughly interlocked with the idea of the preservation of constitutional order and of individual liberty, the two notions which were uppermost in the minds of that generation.

Someone will interpose the objection that,

[1] See, for example, the complaint against "Squire Graball" Hutchinson, because of his holding the office of chief justice while he held that of lieutenant-governor. See Hosmer, *Life of Hutchinson*, 65–68. See also the statement in Massachusetts in 1773, during the discussion between Hutchinson and the legislature, *Writings of Samuel Adams*, II, 429; also the declaration (1772) in the famous paper on the "Rights of the Colonists," where "independent judges" meant "independent as far as possible of prince or people," *ibid.*, 357. Notice too the statements of Dickinson and the struggle in New York and New Jersey.

whatever may have been the theory in the very early days, the system, as provided by the Constitution of the United States or as worked out by the courts, provides for judicial superiority rather than for separation of the powers and distinctness of authority. This may be true; but if the principle of separation has been broken down, is this not due to the fact that the executive and legislative branches have considered themselves bound by the decisions of the courts? Is not the superiority of the courts, if they are now superior, due to general governmental conditions and to the acquiescence of the political departments in court decisions? This acquiescence has been carried to such an extent that, in the vast majority of instances, the political branches appear to accept the conclusions of the court as determining what is constitutional rather than only as an evidence of the opinion of the court and its refusal within its own sphere to act in carrying out a law and making it effective. Is not this acquiescence simply the result of accommodation, the result of an attempt to avoid the inconvenience of conflicting opinions, rather than an essential part of our constitutional system in its theoretical aspects? From a purely theoretical point of view the branches of government are separate.

Theoretically or hypothetically, this separation might result in endless confusion; but such confusion would be simply one of the theoretical and logical results of the principle of the separation of the powers; hence the tendency to recognize the judicial decision as a final determination of what the Constitution is because the court will not participate in carrying out the law. No one is bound by an unconstitutional law; if our constitutional system at the present time includes the principle that the political departments must yield to the decisions of the judiciary on the whole question of constitutionality, such principle is the result of constitutional development and, as I have said, of the acquiescence of the political power because of reasons of expediency and not because they were primarily and originally under the strictest obligation to accept as final more than the decision of the court in the particular case. A large part of our constitutional history is the history of an unconscious attempt to break down or make viable the principle of separation; and as far as the power of the courts is concerned and their relation to other departments, this breaking down or viability has been secured by the readiness of the other branches of government to accept as the Constitution what the court says is the Constitution.

Certainly, whatever the practice may be and whatever may have been the readiness to accept judicial determination as final, it can hardly be said even today that in theory the legislature is controlled in its legislative capacity by the courts. The legislature is not bound by the decision of the court to refrain from passing an act at variance with the court's decision. Such action on the part of the legislature might be unwise, but it is certainly not unconstitutional. When President Jackson, acting in his legislative capacity, vetoed the Bank Bill of 1832, he was undoubtedly within his rights, and so he would have been had he signed a bill providing for an institution which had already been declared unconstitutional by the court. No one can doubt that Congress is not prohibited by the Pollock case from passing an act identically like the Income Tax Act, declared unconstitutional by the Supreme Court. Such congressional action might be unwise or disturbing, but it would not be unconstitutional; and if the personnel of the Supreme Court of the United States has distinctly altered or its opinion and sentiment widened in the last fifteen years, such an act on the part of Congress might be far from unwise. If the assertions I have here made seem extreme—and I can scarcely think they will be so considered—there can be no doubt in anyone's mind that these principles obtained in the early days, when men were working on the principle of the separation of the powers and when judges were asserting their right to independent judgment, in the days before the principle of separation had been partly vitiated by the acquiescence of the political branches.

Before we consider the problem as to whether the President or the executive officers are under obligations in all circumstances to receive from the court the ultimate interpretation of the Constitution and avoid all independent judgment, we need to remind ourselves that no one is bound by an unconstitutional law. To one who has studied through the course of Revolutionary argument, it appears inevitable that the courts in part at least must have viewed the matter in that simple light when they first ventured to declare legislative acts unconstitutional; they looked at the question probably—I say "probably" because this point is hard to demonstrate with absolute certainty—from the viewpoint of the litigant who came to the court for justice, from the viewpoint of the man who had a right to say he was not bound.

Even when we consider the authority of executive officers, the principle at issue is much like that discussed in the preceding paragraph. Is a person or a department of government bound by an unconstitutional act? Everyone will say no, but someone may nevertheless assert that the court determines what is constitutional and what is unconstitutional, and thus, instead of upholding the separation of the powers, the court has assumed control and become the dictator. Can it be said, however, that the President of the United States or any executive officer is controlled by an unconstitutional act? An illustration of what I have in mind is presented by the contests in the Reconstruction period. The reader of Welles's *Diary* will remember how Welles despaired of trying to make General Grant see that he was not under obligations to obey an act if that act was unconstitutional. Grant maintained that he was under obligations to obey a law until the Supreme Court declared it unconstitutional.[1] Such is the natural position of the

[1] "I asked him if Congress could exercise powers not granted, powers that the States, which made the Constitution, had expressly reserved. He thought Congress might pass any law, and the President and all others must obey and support it until the

layman. Such notions as that have distorted our original constitutional system. If the act was unconstitutional, Grant was under no obligations to abide by it. The question was, Was he willing to take the risk that some instrumentality of the government would differ with him?

The President acting in his executive capacity may yield to the opinion of the court and accept its decisions as practically a part of the Constitution; but under the theory of the separation of the powers he is not under strict technical constitutional obligation. He too can interpret the Constitution. This principle is illustrated by the struggle between Johnson and Congress during the Reconstruction time. Secretary Welles, as we have seen, in his interview with Grant made a vain effort to disclose to the military mind the proper principles of constitutional law. Johnson apparently did not need all this explicit explanation. The President is no more bound by an unconstitutional law than is the court. Johnson refused to be bound by the Tenure of Office Act,[1] though

Supreme Court declared it unconstitutional."—*Diary of Gideon Welles*, III, 177.

[1] It is true that Johnson was possibly not acting in direct violation of the Tenure of Office Act when he dismissed Stanton, for Stanton had been appointed by Lincoln. The substantial fact is, however, I think, correctly stated above.

it was passed by a two-thirds vote over his veto. No one probably would deny now that in so refusing he was within his constitutional power.

If these assertions are true, the President in his executive capacity tomorrow would have the strict and technical right to refuse to carry out an act which he believes to be unconstitutional, and in doing so would be simply exercising his right under the principle of the separation of the powers of government and under the principle that nobody is bound by an unconstitutional act. The President can interpret the Constitution. A private citizen will be liable to punishment in case the courts disagree with him. Administrative officers of the government under similar circumstances may find themselves in the same predicament; the President and civil officers of the United States may be subjected to impeachment. The possibility of conflict of opinion between branches of government and the resulting uncertainty or confusion are not unnatural products of the principle of the separation of the powers; and, as I have already asserted, largely because of the disadvantages of this principle, we have to all intents and purposes adopted the doctrine that the Supreme Court does decide what is constitutional and what is not.[1]

Again, it may be, the constitutional principles which I have here just presented may not be acceptable to constitutional jurists. Whether these principles be sound or not is, however, for our purposes not vital; possibly American constitutional law has grown away from its early conditions; the principle of separation and of judicial independence, not judicial superiority, was beyond question distinctly put forth by the judges in the early cases, and on that basis the courts did, as a historical fact, act and assume authority to deny the validity of legislation. Time and again the general principle was laid down by the courts that they were not asserting superiority but only exercising their freedom within their own province.[2]

[1] Those who doubt the power of the court commonly inquire why should *courts* exercise this power; all explanation of the fixity and binding effect of the constitution leaves them unconvinced of the legitimacy of judicial refusal to be bound by legislative enactment. It is only fair to inquire in return why the President or an administrative officer should have the power and the right to act upon the theory of unconstitutionality. Why did Grant have the right to refuse to be bound by an unconstitutional act of Congress? Why was President Johnson at liberty to refuse? Because he was not bound by an unconstitutional act; neither is the court.

[2] See *ante*, pp. 14, 15, 16, 22, 24.

FUNDAMENTAL LAW; REVOLUTIONARY DOCTRINE, 1760–76

If I should account in full measure for the origin and acceptance of the doctrine of the separation of the powers of government, I should in very large measure account for the independent exercise of judicial power, but there would still remain a number of additional conditions and factors to be explained and accounted for. Of prime importance here is the principle that the legislature is bound by the constitution or by the fundamental law. Comment upon this subject is not easy, not because of a paucity of proof or evidence, but because of the mass of it and its demonstrative character. The whole of that generation was influenced by the course of Revolutionary argument; and that argument was thoroughly loaded with the assertions that neither Parliament nor any governmental body was possessed of complete and unlimited authority. The statement of the Declaratory Act of 1766, that the Parliament had the right to bind the colonies in all cases whatsoever, was repeated over and over again in America with words of disapproval that developed into expressions of rebellion. Authorities were cited, arguments were outlined, pamphlets were written, objections were made, against a doctrine of complete legislative supremacy, until every man who walked the streets of an American town must have been firmly convinced of the principle that there were rights and privileges beyond legislative control.

The all-pervading character of that assumption is what I am now endeavoring to emphasize; for if we remember its universal acceptance, we must recognize the fact that the judges were under influence to recognize it when cases arose before them as independent parts of the government. And in this connection it is especially noteworthy that these early cases in general involved questions of individual right and liberty—the right of trial by jury or the right of decent judicial process. If every American in the period under consideration was thoroughly imbued with the belief that legislatures were not omnipotent, if this was the controlling principle of their ordinary thinking on governmental matters, if they believed that an individual was not bound by an unconstitutional act, we cannot expect that the courts would declare that he was so bound, when they had reasonable opportunity in their independent position to recognize and proclaim the fact.

My emphasis, let me say again, is upon the general prevalence and controlling force of this sentiment which was in the foreground of the American Revolution. Largely from these two sentiments, widely if not universally accepted and proclaimed during the Revolution—namely from the doctrine of the separation of the powers and the doctrine that the legislature is not possessed of complete authority—came as a practical fact the assertion of the independent right of the courts to judge whether or not the legislature had transcended its power.

But we have not finished; for there are still many facts and principles to be taken into consideration before the historical background is by any means entirely exposed. Back of this fundamental principle, that legislatures are not possessed of all authority, was the belief in the existence of a fundamental law in the free state—a law which was above all legislative action. This belief was firmly held in the Revolutionary days preceding the adoption of state constitutions. I am speaking of the commonly held beliefs, which emerged in the course of Revolutionary argument, and which led the people to look upon written constitutions as of a sacred and inviolable character,[1] when once they were established. I am not discussing a vague and uncertain notion; I am trying to call adequate attention to a feeling and belief, the depth and strength of which need to be taken into consideration if we would appreciate the fact that they underlay judicial decisions and controlled the judicial mind.

Of course such sentiments as these were peculiarly strong in men like the judges, who had studied the political documents of the Revolutionary time with care and who understood the nature of the American Revolutionary argument. But the common man, of the northern states at least, if not of all the states, must have seen these doctrines of inviolable fundamental law put forth over and over again in the course of discussion. For the central proposition of the Americans was that there was a fundamental law superior to all governmental enactment; they asserted that Parliament was controlled by this fundamental law; the glory of the British constitution was that it embodied fundamental principles of right and justice;

[1] The two principles in fact go hand in hand, if they are not one—the principle that legislatures are bound and the principle that in all free states there is a fundamental law. I have chosen here to distinguish the principles or to analyze the doctrine into its two parts.

and this fundamental law was binding upon Parliament and ought to be binding on all governments.

But the existence of the principle of fundamental law does not necessarily mean that the court has the right to declare an act unconstitutional. This is true; I maintain, however, that, if all men and all officers are thoroughly imbued with this doctrine and recognize it as the controlling principle of the state, nothing can be left for the judges in their judicial capacity except to recognize the fact and the principle. Acting in their independent position, the judges will announce that a law contravening these fundamentals does not bind them or the litigants. Whether the courts *will* or logically *must*, in American history they *did;* and they did so because of the commonly accepted and active principle of American jurisprudence. I do not mean to assert that the courts actually did adopt the practice of declaring laws void because contrary to the fundamental law as long as that law was unwritten and not formally announced in constitutions; my contention is that the continuous declaration that there was a fundamental law necessarily made impression and established a principle and that when the written constitutions were formed and new governments founded, the courts were prepared to put into actual operation the principle of fundamental law.[1]

In this country this principle of the existence of fundamental law was first clearly stated in one of the most popular and influential pamphlets of the early Revolutionary days—Otis' *The Rights of the British Colonies Asserted and Proved* (1764). Otis says among other things, "The supreme legislature cannot justly assume power of ruling by extempore arbitrary decrees, but is bound to dispense justice by known settled rules, and by duly authorized independent judges[2] (p. 55). . . . . These are their

[1] As I point out later, it was a mooted question whether the courts would actually exercise the power of declaring a law void because it violated fundamental principles of justice. But whether they did so or not, the way for the simpler doctrine, the power and duty of the court to declare a law void because contrary to the fundamental law embodied in a written constitution, was prepared by the old assertions of fundamental law, the assertions which played so prominent a part in the whole Revolutionary argument.

[2] Of course the sentiment as here expressed was taken from Locke: "And so, whoever has the legislative or supreme power of any commonwealth, is bound to govern by established standing laws, promulgated and known to the people, and not by extempore decrees, by indifferent and upright judges, who are to decide controversies by those laws."—Second essay, § 131; see also §§ 135, 142, etc.

It may be contended that Locke, whose influence was exceedingly great during the period of the American Revolution and who was very freely and frequently referred to, gave by his

bounds, which by God and nature are fixed, hitherto have they a right to come, and no further. . . . . These are the first principles of law and justice, and the great barriers of a free state, and of the British constitution in particular. To say the parliament is absolute and arbitrary, is a contradiction. The Parliament

writings an argument in favor of the omnipotence of the legislature inasmuch as he so frequently speaks of the extent of legislative authority. It is perfectly plain, however, that the main result of Locke's second treatise on government is the assurance that no government is possessed of supreme and arbitrary authority; to establish that principle his writings were used during the Revolutionary period. Locke's writings are of course of great moment as marking the end of the struggle of the seventeenth century to assert legislative power as over against royal authority, and mark the central point in the rise of the doctrine of parliamentary sovereignty and supremacy. While Locke was maintaining the principle of the authority of Parliament as against the king, he laid down, as I have said, long and substantial arguments against the existence of arbitrary power; and the whole course and drift of his argument was used by the American writers and pamphleteers as conclusive proof of the existence of rights and privileges which were authoritatively binding upon all governmental agencies. The very foundation of the American idea of liberty was that there should be a "standing rule to live by" (Locke, § 22). But the Americans carried this farther than Locke did in some portions of his influential essay. They contended in favor of a law binding on the legislature, while Locke does not always make that principle clear. Compare § 22 and § 222.

"Who are a free people?" said Dickinson. "Not those, over whom government is reasonably and equitably exercised, but those, who live under a government so constitutionally checked and controuled, that proper provision is made against its being otherwise exercised."—Writings of John Dickinson in *Memoirs of the Historical Society of Pennsylvania*, XIV, 356.

cannot make 2 and 2, 5: Omnipotency cannot do it. The supreme power in a state, is *jus dicere* only:—*jus dare*, strictly speaking, belongs alone to God" (p. 70). It is, however, unnecessary to multiply quotations, although it is only by reading these contemporary documents that one can get anything like a comprehensive impression as to the extent to which men appealed to this principle.

No one who knows anything of the Revolution can doubt the immense influence of James Otis and his writings in forming opinion and the basis for argument and theory. I am inclined to think that Otis was in large measure responsible for the main drift of the documents put forward by Massachusetts in 1768, which were doubtless known to the reading public in America. One of these documents, the Circular Letter, was, of course, widely distributed, and probably every lawyer and politician, from one end of the land to the other, knew its contents and was familiar with its principles. The Circular Letter contains the central element of the American argument in the Revolution. This letter declares "That in all free States the Constitution is fixd; and as the supreme Legislative derives its Power and Authority from the Constitution, it cannot overleap the

Bounds of it without destroying its own foundation: That the Constitution ascertains and limits both Sovereignty and allegiance, and therefore, his Majestys American Subjects who acknowledge themselves bound by the Ties of Allegiance, have an equitable Claim to the full enjoym[t] of the fundamental Rules of the British Constitution. That it is an essential, unalterable Right in nature, ingrafted into the British Constitution, as a fundamental Law . . . . that what a man has honestly acquird is absolutely his own . . . . "[1]

The other letters of which I have spoken reiterate this doctrine of fundamental law. "The supreme legislative, in every free state, derives its power from the constitution; by the fundamental rules of which, it is bounded and circumscribed" (*ibid.*, 134). "There are, my Lord, fundamental rules of the constitution, which, it is humbly presumed, neither the supreme legislative nor the supreme executive can alter. In all free states, the constitution is fixed; it is from thence, that the legislative derives its authority; therefore it cannot change the constitution without destroying its own foundation" (*ibid.*, 156). "But, in all free states, the constitution is fixed; it is from

[1] *Writings of Samuel Adams*, I, 185.

thence, that the supreme legislative, as well as the supreme executive derives its authority. Neither, then, can break through the fundamental rules of the constitution, without destroying their own foundation" (*ibid.*, 170).[1]

Perhaps these citations are alone sufficient to establish my assertion that a central cardinal element of American contention against Great Britain was that the legislature could not overstep its authority and that such principles were firmly fixed in the English system. It was characteristic of the American Revolution that, as in other English revolutions, men contended that they already possessed rights and privileges, which in reality they were seeking to establish.

The Circular Letter and the other letters or documents of 1768, which have just been quoted, were probably drafted by Samuel Adams, but, as I have said, the line of argument

[1] Similar expression found *ibid.*, pp. 174 and 175, 180, 190, 196. See for fundamental principles, "Rights of the Colonists," *ibid.*, II, 350 ff. See also *ibid.*, 452, where the House of Representatives in Massachusetts is engaged in this famous argument with Hutchinson: "Your Excellency has not thought proper, to attempt to confute the reasoning of a learned writer on the laws of nature and of nations, quoted by us on this occasion, to shew that the authority of the Legislature does not extend so far as the fundamentals of the constitution . . . .", etc. See also *ibid.*, 325 (1772), with references to Vattel and Locke.

was probably furnished by Otis. Once again we are led back to Otis' widely read pamphlet, and there we find the source of his statement.[1] He gives an excerpt from Vattel's *Law of Nature and of Nations*. Speaking of the legislative power Vattel says: "It is here demanded whether, if their power extends so far as to the fundamental laws, they may change the constitution of the state? The principles we have laid down lead us to decide this point with certainty, that the authority of these legislators does not extend so far, and that they ought to consider the fundamental laws as sacred, if the nation has not in very express terms given them the power to change them. For the constitution of the state ought to be fixed; and since that was first established by the nation, which afterwards trusted certain persons with the legislative power, the fundamental laws are excepted from their commission." In another portion of the paragraph from which Otis quoted these words—in fact in the very next sentence—Vattel says, "In short, it is from the constitution that those legislators derive their power: how then can they change it

[1] Otis, *Rights of the Colonists*, 109. The words quoted appear in Otis' pamphlet, in a footnote to a memorial transmitted by the Massachusetts House to their agent in England.

without destroying the foundation of their own authority?"

Naturally these assertions and this idea were taken up and expressed by the courts, and the source is evident. Whether they gathered the statement of the principle first from the Circular Letter or from Otis' pamphlet is immaterial. In the case of *Bayard* vs. *Singleton*[1] and in Varnum's argument in *Trevett* vs. *Weeden*, two of the cases already referred to among the state decisions between 1776 and 1787, we find the assertion that the legislature cannot violate the constitution without destroying its own foundation. Varnum quoted at length from Vattel.

[1] James Iredell of North Carolina, who became a federal judge after the founding of the federal government, was strongly of the opinion that a court had the power and the duty to declare a law void. He was much interested in the case of *Bayard* vs. *Singleton* and his letters at that time (1786–87), one a public letter printed in the press, fully discloses the line of thought. It was consonant in most respects with that of Otis on the fundamental law. Judging from Iredell's expression, one would believe he had read Vattel. See especially McKee, *Life and Corr. of Iredell*, II, 173. His letter discloses the intimate connection between this argument in defense of the court's right and the experiences of the Revolution: "We were not ignorant of the theory of the necessity of the legislature being absolute in all cases, because it was the great ground of the British pretenses" (*ibid.*, 146). "Without an express Constitution the powers of the legislature would undoubtedly have been absolute (as the Parliament of Great Britain is held to be), and any act passed, *not inconsistent with natural justice* (for that curb is avowed by the judges even in

NATURAL RIGHTS: THE PERIOD FROM 1760–76

The Americans asserted that men were possessed of certain natural rights which no government could take away. It was the glory of the British constitution that it maintained and assured these rights. Modern writers and readers appear not to appreciate the strength and nature of the natural-right argument. Limitations arising from natural rights were looked upon by the men of the Revolution as *legal* limitations. When they said that Parliament had no authority to disregard natural rights, they did not mean that it was morally wrong or cruel or unjust, but that such disregard was beyond the competence of Parliament or any other body possessing governmental authority.[1] Natural law protecting

England), would have been binding on the people. The experience of the evils which the American war fully disclosed, attending an absolute power in a legislative body, suggested the propriety of a real, original contract between the people and this future government, such, perhaps, as there has been no instance of in the world but in America" (*ibid.*, 172). The whole of these letters should be carefully read, for Iredell had as much influence probably as anyone, possibly more than anyone, in maintaining the doctrine of judicial power. His words show, as I have said, that the power of the court was a product of Revolutionary experiences and of Revolutionary argument.

[1] The remarks of Professor Thayer on this subject appear to be peculiarly deficient in appreciation of the vitality of this belief. The colonists were not arguing that there were certain

natural rights was law and should be recognized by every governmental functionary. They maintained, over and over again, that Englishmen had a constitution and that that constitution embodied principles of natural justice which were beyond the reach of legislative action, a constitution which was fixed and unalterable by legislative enactment and above legislative caprice. Once more, we must evaluate fully the strength of this contention and the force of this argument, to understand the mental background and the legal thinking of statesmen and lawyers of the Revolutionary period and of the years immediately following.

Even if we could refer to no particular and precise declarations, made in the days of Revolutionary argument, 1760–76, that courts of law are under obligations to refuse to con-

vague notions of justice which it would be wrong to disregard; they asserted that they had rights and that these rights could not legally be taken away. They were not rebels; they were preserving constitutional limitations. Compare J. B. Thayer, *Legal Essays* 6, 7. It ought not to be difficult to conceive of colonists and lawyers, acquainted with the common law, insisting on the binding character of principles of right. The principles of justice, which were supposed to be the glory of the common law, were daily announced by courts; to give expression to them was in considerable degree the function of the common-law courts. In cases not involving the validity of legislation we still see courts deciding cases at common law on the ground that to decide otherwise would be to disregard natural justice.

sider valid any legislative act violating the fundamental law or encroaching upon reserved natural rights, we might still be ready to assert that, when the time came and opportunity offered, courts would be likely to announce and apply those principles, especially in extreme cases, where fundamental rights were encroached upon by legislative act, and, more especially still, where those fundamental rights had distinct guaranty in the written constitution. The student of American constitutional law knows full well that it long remained a question whether the courts would not recognize principles of natural justice and the existence of natural right as constituting direct limitations upon legislative authority, even where no special constitutional prohibition was involved. For some time, after the adoption of the state constitutions, there was uncertainty as to whether the courts would content themselves with looking on the written constitution as a law emanating from the people and therefore binding on the legislature; it was uncertain whether they would not go farther, even to the extent of maintaining natural rights which were not explicitly protected by constitutional guaranty. It is plain too that the courts were relieved from this difficulty by the bills of rights constituting express constitutional limitations, to which the courts could give wide bearing as limitations upon interference with natural rights and justice.[1] Such an attitude on the part of the courts was a product of the prevalence of the Revolutionary opinion that natural law was real *law*, that natural justice was a real constitutional limitation, and that the legislative body in every free state is limited by fundamental principles of individual right and liberty.

I have said that, even if there were, in the early Revolutionary period, no reference to the duty of the courts to declare acts contrary to natural justice or to fundamental law void and of no effect, so deep and assured was this feeling and so strong was the principle, that we might expect the courts to act accordingly, when once Americans courts, American legislatures, and American law were established. Such a judicial position would have been a natural product of Revolutionary opinion. But as a matter of fact, there were a number of such references to just such judicial power and

[1] The broad general statements of the bills of rights, especially the one about "due process of law," enabled the courts to assume the position that they enforced only the written law; but they held that those rights existed anterior to the state, and they recognized those rights as constitutionally secured by these blanket provisions of the constitution.

obligation. The currency of this notion was doubtless due in the first place to Otis' famous speech on the Writs of Assistance, in which he maintained that the courts would pass such an act of Parliament "into disuse." Such a notion, backed by Otis' almost unbounded popularity and fiery zeal, took hold of the thought and imagination of the New England men. Again in Otis' pamphlet to which I have already referred, which was doubtless read with great interest on both sides of the water, we find a like declaration. "If the reasons," he says, "that can be given against an act, are such as plainly demonstrate that it is against *natural* equity, the executive courts will adjudge such act void. It may be questioned by some, though I make no doubt of it, whether they are not obliged by their oaths to adjudge such acts void."[1] In the appendix to this pamphlet appears the substance of a memorial presented to the House of Representatives in Massachusetts in pursuance of the instructions of Boston to its representatives; and in this

[1] Otis said in his speech against writs of assistance: "As to Acts of Parliament, an Act against the Constitution is void: an Act against natural Equity is void: and if an Act of Parliament should be made, in the very Words of this Petition, it would be void. The Executive Courts must pass such Acts into disuse—8. Rep. 118. from Viner.—Reason of ye Com Law to control an Act of Parliament." Quincy's Reports (Mass.) 474.

connection we find references to the cases in the English courts and the opinions of justices declaring that acts of Parliament made against natural equity are void: "The judges of England have declared in favour of these sentiments, when they expressly declare, that acts of parliament against natural equity are void. That acts against the fundamental principles of the British constitution are void."

John Adams, in making his plea to the governor in council asking that the courts of justice should be allowed to go on without reference to the Stamp Act, said: "The Stamp Act, I take it, is utterly void and of no binding force upon us; for it is against our Rights as Men and our Privileges as Englishmen. An Act made in Defiance of the first Principles of Justice. . . . . Parliaments may err; they are not infallible; they have been refused to be submitted to. An Act making the King's Proclamation to be Law, the Executive Power adjudged absolutely void. . . . . There are certain Principles fixed unalterably in Nature."[1] Otis made an extended argument as a colleague

[1] Quincy Reports 200. In 1765 Hutchinson said, speaking of opposition of the Stamp Act, "The prevailing reason at this time is, that the Act of Parliament is against Magna Charta, and the natural Rights of Englishmen, and therefore, according to Lord Coke, null and void."—Quincy's Reports (Mass.) 527, note.

of Adams. Referring to Malloy, *De Jure Mar.*, he said, "the Laws which forbid a Man to pursue his Right one Way, ought to be understood with this equitable Restriction, that one finds Judges to whom he may apply. When there are no Courts of Law to appeal to, it is then we must have Recourse to the Law of Nature."[1]

There can be no doubt that such cases and opinions as Otis gives, in the pamphlet above

[1] *Ibid.*, 204. "His Excellency the Governour" expressed this opinion: "The Arguments made Use of, both by Mr. Adams and you, would be very pertinent to induce the Judges of the Superiour Court to think the Act of no Validity, and that therefore they should pay no Regard to it; but the Question with me is whether that very Thing don't argue the Impropriety of our Intermeddling in a Matter which solely belongs to them to judge of in their Judicial Department" (*ibid.*, 206).

Governor Hutchinson in writing to Jackson, agent of the province in England, after saying that he thought that the Stamp Act must be valid because Parliament passed it, said "but our friends to liberty take advantage of a maxim they find in Lord Coke that an act of Parliament against Magna Charta or the peculiar rights of Englishmen is *ipso facto* void."—Quincy's Reports 441; see also *ibid.*, 444–45.

It is interesting to notice that Quincy, who was the reporter of the important decisions in the volume above referred to, wrote "qu"—that is, query—opposite the statements of the power of Parliament in Blackstone's *Commentaries*, I, 49, 97, 161, 189, and made references to Vattel's *Law of Nations*, Book I, chap. iii, pp. 15–19, and to Furneaux's Letter to Blackstone. See the notes in Quincy's Reports 527.

In a case before the General Court of Virginia in 1772 George Mason, as reported by Thomas Jefferson, argued that the provi-

referred to, were very familiar to the lawyers of that time who were conversant with the decisions of the English courts and with the great text-writers on English law. While it cannot be proved as a mathematical demonstration that all well-read lawyers at that period were familiar with these decisions and opinions, it is a reasonable or inevitable inference; but if they were not familiar, the quotations and citations which Otis gave should be sufficient to introduce them to the main principle. Concerning the background of such principles as this, namely the right of the court to pass an act of Parliament into disuse, I shall have something to say farther on. I am now confining my attention to what was palpably present in the minds of the men of the early Revolutionary days and to those general principles which must have taken strong hold on lawyers and judges

sion of the statutes of the Colony of 1682 that "all Indians which shall hereafter be sold by our neighboring Indians . . . . are hereby adjudged, deemed and taken to be slaves" was "originally void, because contrary to natural right and justice," and cited Coke and Hobart.—*Robin et al.* vs. *Hardaway et al.*, Jefferson (Va.) Reports 109, 113.

The character of the legal references to which the men of the time used to support their position that an act of Parliament made against natural equity would be void, can be seen from the references made in Otis' *Rights of the Colonies Asserted and Proved*, 110, note. From these references it is evident that Otis had carefully followed and examined the English authorities.

and affected their opinions, when they came to the point of interpreting American constitutions and building up the system of American constitutional law.

The function of common-law courts of declaring what the law is frequently involves in reality the duty of asserting the fundamental principles of justice which appeal to the court as part and parcel of the law. In the earlier days, and more or less ever since, the courts have professed, even when actually engaged in the making of law, to be engaged in the announcement of the maxims of substantial justice which were known to the law.[1] It was much

[1] To one who is not bound by the chains of mathematical logic and is not looking only for technically legal precedents, the practice of courts of interpreting statutes in the light of common-law principles, of torturing statutes almost out of recognition into conformity with the principles of justice or, as the old English judges might have said, into conformity with dictates of reason and the common law, is of value in any effort to understand the attitude of courts to legislation and to natural right. Such juggling with statutes was only the half-way house to a full refusal to accept and apply the statute. We see, for example, in *Page* vs. *Pendleton et al.* (1793) (Wythe [Va.] Reports 211, Court of Chancery) an evident determination to enforce justice and natural right. "If this," says Judge Wythe in a note, "seems contrary to what is called authority . . . . the publisher of the opinion will be against the authority, when, in a question depending, like the present, on the law of nature, the authority is against reason, which is affirmed to be the case here." At considerable pains and trouble the court reaches the conclusion that because the legislature had no right to do a certain thing, the legislature

easier for a common-law court to bring in and apply such principles and thus in a way to build up a great body of right, than would have been the case, had the courts been, from time immemorial, accustomed only to interpret and apply written legislative enactment.

In attempting to account for the legal and constitutional principles considered by judges to be the fundamental principle of American law, we have thus far noticed a series of facts and of sentiments of vital importance when America was setting up her principles of government as over against the English Parliamentarian: (1) the fact that the main contention of the Americans was that Parliament was not possessed of absolute authority; (2) the belief that there were certain principles of right and justice which all governments must consider and that the obligation to consider them

could not have intended to do what it probably did intend to do. But in the course of the discussion the court says (p. 215): "If the parliament of Great-britain should, by an act, declare the rights of creditors, of any other, or all other countries, to money due from british subjects, to be extinguished, all courts, perhaps those of Westminster hall not excepted, would adjure [abjure] such legislative omnipotence arrogated by the parliament, but that parliament hath not less power than any other legislature." This is an indication that even as late as 1793, an American lawyer could believe Parliament not possessed of legislative omnipotence and could believe the English courts possessed power to reject an act of Parliament.

constituted a legal limitation on governmental authority; (3) the assertion that these fundamentals were embodied in the English constitution, which was fundamental and unchangeable because it embodied these fundamental and unchangeable principles; (4) the conviction that the courts were under obligations to declare void an act of Parliament violating the principles of natural justice and reason, a conviction supported by reference to English decisions and opinions of great judges; (5) a declaration, closely connected with the preceding, that there is a fundamental law which the legislature cannot change, a principle, however, which did not come by any means solely through a perusal of English authority and legal decisions, but from text-writers of continental Europe who embodied the principles of philosophic thinking. I shall now proceed to consider more fully the legal and philosophical background, first referring to the principles of the English law and next to the general principles of continental publicists.

FUNDAMENTAL LAW; ENGLISH AND CONTINENTAL BACKGROUND

If we should seek for the beginnings of the principle in English history that there was a fundamental law of the constitution, our way would lead us well back into the Middle Ages; we should need to consider the characteristics of feudalism, and, back of all that, the primitive regard for unchanging custom. It is naturally impossible for us to attempt any such task in a paper of this kind. I must refer my readers to the admirable chapter on "Fundamental Law" in Professor McIlwain's book, *The High Court of Parliament*, where the extent and character of this belief is traced from early times down through the seventeenth century. Professor McIlwain's chapter is a signal contribution; and yet we doubtless remember that we were all brought up to think that the Englishmen, in the course of constitutional development, were continually insisting, not so much upon new rights, as on the recognition of the old and established principles of freedom. This assertion of a fundamental law above the king was made over and over again in the course of passing centuries; and it appeared also in books to which the American colonies had access.[1]

[1] Magna Charta came to be viewed as unalterable. "It was not Magna Carta," says Professor Adams, "but the circumstances of the future which gave to the fact that there was a body of law above the king creative power in English history. .... The great work of Magna Carta was not done by its specific provisions; the secret of its influence is to be found in its underlying idea."—*Am. Hist. Rev.*, XIII, 238, n. There is evidence also of the

In the early activities of Parliament the notion prevailed that it was the business of Parliament rather to declare the law than make new laws; and in this respect the activity of Parliament was not markedly distinct from that of the courts; neither Parliament nor court were engaged in passing new law but in declaring

recognition of the fundamental law not necessarily embodied in Magna Charta.

How far back in American history this notion can be traced is evidenced in some degree by the facts that gave rise to the Body of Liberties. The colonists of Massachusetts, in fear of the growth of unrestrained government, desired something in the nature of a Magna Charta. The Body of Liberties, it is true, was drawn up and announced by the General Court apparently under popular pressure; the laws were intended to guide and limit the magistrates; but it seems plain that the people wanted the law fixed and feared governmental power. The intimate connection between the principles of New England and the contemporary struggles of old England is evident, as is also the American inheritance of the idea of fundamental law. "The deputies having conceived great danger to our state, in regard that our magistrates, for want of positive laws, in many cases, might proceed according to their discretions, it was agreed that some men should be appointed to frame a body of grounds of laws, in resemblance to a Magna Charta, which, being allowed by some of the ministers, and the general court, should be received for fundamental laws."—*Winthrop's Journal*, I, 151 (Hosmer's ed.).

"The people had long desired a body of laws, and thought their condition very unsafe, while so much power rested in the discretion of magistrates. Divers attempts had been made at former courts, and the matter referred to some of the magistrates and some of the elders; but still it came to no effect; for, being committed to the care of many, whatsoever was done by some, was still disliked or neglected by others. At last it was referred to Mr. Cotton and Mr. Nathaniel Warde, etc., and each of them

the old and especially fundamental law. When the great contest came on between Charles I and Parliament, the question at first was not whether Parliament or the king should rule but whether the king should be held bound by fundamental law. "All our Petition," said Pym, "is for the Laws of *England*, and this Power seems to be another distinct Power from the Power of the Law: I know how to add Sovereign to his Person, but not to his Power: and we cannot leave to him a Sovereign Power: Also we never were possessed of it."

framed a model, which were presented to this general court, and by them committed to the governor and deputy and some others to consider of, and so prepare it for the court in the 3d month next. Two great reasons there were, which caused most of the magistrates and some of the elders not to be very forward in this matter. One was, want of sufficient experience of the nature and disposition of the people, considered with the condition of the country and other circumstances, which made them conceive, that such laws would be fittest for us, which should arise pro re nata upon occasions, etc., *and so the laws of England and other states grew, and therefore the fundamental laws of England are called customs, consuetudines* [italics not in original]. 2. For that it would professedly transgress the limits of our charter, which provide, we shall make no laws repugnant to the laws of England, and that we were assured we must do. But to raise up laws by practice and custom had been no transgression; as in our church discipline, and in matters of marriage, to make a law, that marriages should not be solemnized by ministers, is repugnant to the laws of England; but to bring it to a custom by practice for the magistrates to perform it, is no law made repugnant, etc. At length (to satisfy the people) it proceeded, and the two models

Everyone knows that in the course of the great English rebellion, as Parliamentary power developed, men began to consider how they could place limits even on the power of Parliament. This problem was one of consuming interest and of great perplexity to those who were troubled by the difficulties of the time, especially by the troubles arising between 1647 and 1654 or 1655; we all know too that the Instrument of Government definitely asserted that certain provisions should be forever unalterable. The controversy between Parliament and the king, the events of the years of the Restoration, and the establishment of a

were digested with divers alterations and additions, and abbreviated and sent to every town, (12,) to be considered of first by the magistrates and elders, and then to be published by the constables to all the people, that if any man should think fit, that any thing therein ought to be altered, he might acquaint some of the deputies herewith against the next court."—*Ibid.*, 323–24.

"This session continued three weeks, and established 100 laws, which were called the *Body of Liberties*. They had been composed by Mr. Nathaniel Ward, (sometime pastor of the church of Ipswich: he had been a minister in England, and formerly a student and practiser in the course of the common law,) and had been revised and altered by the court, and sent forth into every town to be further considered of, and now again in this court, they were revised, amended, and presented, and so established for three years, by that experience to have them fully amended and established to be perpetual."—*Ibid.*, II, 48–49.

The steps taken to secure the approbation of the people indicate that these laws were intended to be fundamental and unchanging. The General Court was in theory the whole corporation—the commonwealth.

new monarch by Parliamentary authority in the Revolution of 1688, mark the foundation of the fact of Parliamentary sovereignty and supremacy, a fact which soon became a constitutional theory. The constitutional question, in other words, in the middle years of the great Rebellion, was whether fundamental law could be established, recognized, and enforced against the new sovereign, the Parliament. This was the thought that perplexed the army, and this thought was back of the Agreement of the People and the Heads of Proposals.[1] One who would understand the development of American principles of government and constitutional law must bear in mind that the English colonies separated from England

[1] See *The Clarke Papers* (Camden Society); W. Rothschild, *Der Gedanke der geschriebenen Verfassung in der Englischen Revolution*. It is only necessary to remember that the New England colonies were the fruit of the English Rebellion in its early phases, and that English and American Independents were not distinctly separated for years after the early settlement, to understand why the idea of fundamental law in the nature of a Magna Charta should be the demand of the New England men.

The Americans, irrespective of their charters, which they sometimes looked on as peculiarly fundamental, obtained this doctrine (*a*) from the assertion they found in the books; (*b*) from their retrospection on English history; (*c*) as a special inheritance through colonial history from the days of the early seventeenth century. The New England Puritans were moreover of course desirous of maintaining the law of God and the Scriptures as superior to human enactment.

rather in the seventeenth century than in the eighteenth century, and that they carried forward in their thinking and embodied in their institutions the principles of liberty and government that were struggled for by the advanced party of the great rebellion.

The American colonists, therefore, when they contested the power of Parliament, had behind them many centuries of English doctrine, while the supremacy or sovereignty of Parliament was comparatively new. Moreover, as I have said, in the books and cases to which these men referred, they could find much expression of the existence of fundamental law, and they thus obtained the written approval of the stand which they were desirous to take against Parliament. The importance of that position and the significance of the colonial argument are of great interest when we remember that, in 1765, Parliament, practically for the first time in a noticeable way, was asserting absolute sovereignty as characteristic of its imperial power and authority.

If I have sufficiently emphasized the great fact that Englishmen had asserted over and over again for centuries that there was a fundamental law of the land and also the fact that such assertion appeared in the books which colonial lawyers read,[1] it need not surprise us to find that the American lawyers took up that doctrine in the controversies against Great Britain and were prepared to make it a most vital and determinative principle in the interpretation of the written constitution. Here we find the actual, vital development of a great race instinct and ideal.

The notion of fundamental law, however, was not confined to Englishmen alone or to the English publicists. It appeared in the writings

[1] The following statements in Gray's notes on the writ of assistance admirably sum up the facts: "But Otis, while he recognized the jurisdiction of Parliament over the Colonies, denied that it was the final arbiter of the justice and constitutionality of its own acts; and relying upon words of the greatest English lawyers, and putting out of sight the circumstances under which they were uttered, contended that the validity of statutes must be judged by the Courts of Justice; and thus foreshadowed the principle of American Constitutional Law, that it is the duty of the judiciary to declare unconstitutional statutes void.

"His main reliance was the well-known statement of Lord Coke in Dr. Bonham's case—It appeareth in our books, that in many cases the common law will control Acts of Parliament and adjudge them to be utterly void; for where an Act of Parliament is against common right and reason or repugnant or impossible to be performed, the common law will control it and adjudge it to be void. Otis seems also to have had in mind the equally familiar *dictum* of Lord Hobart—Even an Act of Parliament made against natural equity, as to make a man judge in his own case, is void in itself: for *jura naturae sunt immutabilia*, and they are *leges legum*. Lord Holt is reported to have said, What my Lord Coke says in Dr. Bonham's case in his 8 Rep. is far from any extravagancy, for it is a very reasonable and true saying,

of continental theorists who were endeavoring to map out a system of government and to intimate that government was for the good of mankind and should not be entirely arbitrary. Once again we should be carried far back along the pathway of history, should we attempt to trace the development or the assertions of this principle; this I shall not attempt to do. I will content myself with pointing again to those assertions of Vattel[1] to which I have already

That if an Act of Parliament should ordain that the same person should be party and judge, or what is the same thing, judge in his own cause, it would be a void Act of Parliament.

"The law was laid down in the same way, on the authority of the above cases, in Bacon's Abridgement, first published in 1735; in Viner's Abridgment, published 1741–51, from which Otis quoted it; and in Comyn's Digest, published 1762–67, but written more than twenty years before. And there are older authorities to the same effect. So that at the time of Otis' agreement [argument] his position appeared to be supported by some of the highest authorities in the English law.

"The same doctrine was repeatedly asserted by Otis and was a favorite in the Colonies before the Revolution. There are later *dicta* of many eminent judges to the effect that a statute may be void as exceeding the just limits of legislative power; but it is believed there is no instance, except one case in South Carolina, in which an act of the legislature has been set aside by the courts, except for conflict with some written constitutional provision."—Quincy's (Mass.) Reports, 1761–72, Appendix, 520–29. The South Carolina case is the case of *Bowman* vs. *Middleton* already referred to, 1 Bay (S.C.) 252.

[1] Vattel's volume appeared in 1758 and was almost immediately translated into English. He is referred to over and over again by the American pamphleteers and he was long looked upon in

referred; the notion was of course not original with Vattel. It was the characteristic of the American Revolutionists that they took theories of popular right and of governmental obligation with great seriousness and earnestness—one might better say with literalness—and believed that they were making effective, and were called upon to make effective, these great philosophic principles of substantial justice. They did not believe they were creating them.

NATURAL RIGHT: ENGLISH AND CONTINENTAL BACKGROUND

Closely allied, as I have already said, with the doctrine of fundamental law was the notion of

America as a fundamental authority. Next to him Grotius and Pufendorf appear to be more commonly referred to than any other continental publicists. Among the other references to Vattel may be mentioned: *Writings of Samuel Adams*, II, 258, 323, 325; *Life and Writings of Franklin* (Macmillan ed.), VI, 432; I, 142, n; *Writings of Madison* (Cong. ed.), I, 129, 578, 651; II, 249, 309; 1 Dallas (Pa.) 113; 2, 234 (1795); 3 Dallas (1794) 2; N. J. Reports I, 117 (1791). These references are only indications of familiarity with Vattel.

There appears to be a general impression that the authors referred to by the colonists were Blackstone and Montesquieu and possibly Rousseau. Men like Wilson referred to the great continental publicists freely; and John Adams left a statement concerning his reading of them. In my judgment it would be a great mistake to include Rousseau at all among those that particularly influenced the men of the Revolution, as it would also be to suppose that Blackstone was followed when his remarks did not fit in with Revolutionary theory.

natural right. This, too, the colonists took literally and with great seriousness. Fundamental law was primarily the embodiment of natural justice and reason. The limits of reason and of natural justice they considered as legal limits upon governmental action and their notion of fundamental law was strengthened and confirmed by all they read of the existence of natural rights. To understand the full force of this theory we need to remember how frequently, how almost universally, this fact of natural right appears in the writings of great publicists of the two centuries before the Revolution, and we need to remember especially the influence of the Reformation, of Calvinism, and of Puritanism in begetting the notion that men were subject primarily to the law of God. But when once we get clearly in our minds this broad historical background and this politico-theological doctrine, when once we realize that Puritanism and Puritanic thinking were not dead in New England, even in the period when the lawyer and the politician were taking the place of the minister and the church-teacher as public leaders and guiders of public faith, we shall see how it came that these fundamental notions of individual rights, antedating all government and superior to all human authority, dominated the thinking of men in practical affairs of politics.[1]

A quotation from Wilson's law lectures amply illustrates my main contention. Commenting upon the right of Parliament, he speaks as follows: "'I know of no power,' says Sir William Blackstone, 'which can control the parliament.' His meaning is obviously, that he knew no *human* power sufficient for this purpose. But the parliament may, unquestionably, be controlled by natural or revealed law, proceeding from *divine* authority. Is not this authority superior to any thing that can be enacted by parliament? Is not this superior authority binding upon the courts of justice?

[1] Pollock, in his *Expansion of the Common Law* (p. 121), says: "It was a current opinion among the mediaeval doctors that rules of positive municipal law were controlled by the law of nature, and not binding if they were contrary to it; though some advocates of the Emperor's independent authority in secular matters, as against the claim of universal supremacy for the Pope, avoided inconvenient consequences by tempering the general proposition with a rather strong presumption that the acts of the lawful sovereign were right. Opposition to princes and rulers in vindication of the law of nature was possible, but at the opposer's peril if he were mistaken, and not to be lightly entered upon."

There can be no doubt of the longevity of this doctrine and of its having leaked down through the passing ages to the men of the American Revolution. The doctrine was always taking on new forms, getting new impetus from new ideas and from new necessities; but it continued and found its ultimate place of rest and of influence in American bills of rights enforced by courts.

When repugnant commands are delivered by two different authorities, one inferior and the other superior; which must be obeyed? When the courts of justice obey the superior authority, it cannot be said with propriety that they control the inferior one; they only declare, as it is their duty to declare, that this inferior one is controlled by the other, which is superior. They do not repeal the act of parliament: they pronounce it void, because contrary to an overruling law. From that overruling law, they receive the authority to pronounce such a sentence. In this derivative view, their sentence is of obligation paramount to the act of the inferior legislative power.

"In the United States, the legislative authority is subjected to another control, beside that arising from natural and revealed law; it is subjected to the control arising from the constitution. From the constitution, the legislative department, as well as every other part of government, derives its power; by the constitution, the legislative, as well as every other department, must be directed; of the constitution, no alteration by the legislature can be made or authorized. In our system of jurisprudence, these positions appear to be incontrovertible. The constitution is the supreme law of the land: to that supreme law every other power must be inferior and subordinate. . . . .

"This regulation is far fron throwing any disparagement upon the legislative authority of the United States. It does not confer upon the judicial department a power superior, in its general nature, to that of the legislature; but it confers upon it, in particular instances, and for particular purposes, the power of declaring and enforcing the superior power of the constitution—the supreme law of the land."[1]

An examination of these sentences of Wilson's lectures will make apparent to anyone the main route followed by American lawyers. No one has doubt of Wilson's ability as a lawyer. No one can read his lectures and not be impressed with his learning and his knowledge of the great writers on law and political philosophy. He takes issue in various places with Blackstone; in these particular sentences he contends that the legislature is bound by divine law, i.e., by natural law; that courts can consequently declare a law encroaching on natural justice void, and that the duty of

[1] Wilson's *Works* (Andrews' ed.), II, 415. I cannot be absolutely sure that this lecture was actually delivered. From the introduction to the first edition of Wilson's lectures (1804) I should judge that some of the lectures were not delivered.

American courts is made doubly imperative by written constitutions which are law. After reading these words it is needless to deny that the American judges reached their position along the old, well-worn route of natural justice and fundamental law—the English route—and were guided and instructed by the great continental European publicists who constantly proclaimed natural right. Wilson was one of the three federal judges who, in the "first Hayburn case," in April, 1792, just about the time when the lecture above quoted was given, declared a law of Congress unconstitutional.

COLONIAL EXPERIENCE: THE ENGLISH EMPIRE

To make this study anything like complete, even in outline—and I have attempted little more—I should probably include certain other institutional facts of historical growth to which I have not referred. I may pass over these facts somewhat hastily because they do not demand extended comment and because they have so frequently been mentioned in discussions of this subject. The facts I refer to are the general character of colonial institutions and the practices of the English empire. A number of the colonies retained charters of government throughout colonial days. Two of these colonies were distinctly established as corporations with corporation charters, and, though the theory was apparently not very active, the principle that acts in excess of legislative authority are void, like any act of a corporation in excess of its authority, must, we may surmise, have had some effect on the legal mind. Moreover, there never had been in America a legislative body possessed of all power; this fact, like so many others that I have mentioned, probably helped to constitute the psychological if not the legal basis for the position afterward taken by the state courts in declaring state acts contrary to the constitution invalid.

To this institutional fact, the existence of fixed charters, we must add the right of the king in council to annul the enactments of colonial legislatures and thus to maintain the imperial system. This right of annulment, it will be contended, was of executive or legislative character, rather than judicial. I am not sure that there is any validity in insisting that this sharp distinction, which we now make between executive and judicial power, was applicable to colonial times. Such distinctions came only slowly into relief. But, however that may be, the annulment of legislative acts by an authority outside of the legislature must be taken into consideration if only for the reason that it emphasized the absence of legislative omnipotence and the absence of finality in legislative action. Such annulment might be on the ground that the legislature had acted unjustly or on the ground that it had transcended its charter limits or passed an act repugnant to the law in England. To this annulment by the king in council we must add in our view of the background the instances of appeal from colonial courts to the king in council; for in these cases there was a distinct exercise of judicial authority, and in some of them the validity of colonial legislation was in dispute.[1] When the time came to form the Union under the Constitution, men placed upon state courts the obligation to regard the Constitution as law; and it is not at all unlikely that this use of the courts to preserve order in the *federal*

[1] Professor Thayer, for example, in his *Legal Essays*, appears to derive the power of the courts to declare a law unconstitutional chiefly from the power of the king in council during colonial times.

There are some well-known cases of appeal where the validity of important colonial laws was brought directly into question, notably *Winthrop* vs. *Lechmere*, *Phillips* vs. *Savage*, *Clark* vs. *Tousey*. Between 1735 and 1776 there appear to have been fifty-nine cases adjudicated by the king in council brought up on appeal from Rhode Island alone. For this whole matter see H. D. Hazeltine, "Appeals from Colonial Courts to the King in Council, with Special Reference to Rhode Island," *Am. Hist. Assoc. Annual Report*, 1894, 299 ff.

system—in the federal empire—was an inheritance from the colonial system in which the authority of the British Council was used for preserving imperial order.[1]

Probably this historical background—colonial experience, the nature and the practices of the imperial system—had its effect. Much of our federal system, much of our general political order, came from colonial history and from the workings of the British empire. But while this is true, and while from these antecedents may have come some of the influences, which led to the power of the courts to declare laws void, the main line of argument and the main ideas on which the courts took their stand arose during the course of Revolutionary discussion. The ideas were an inheritance from England; they were supported by references to English judges and to principles of natural justice and right; and they were strengthened by principles and theories of European publicists. Without this colonial experience the courts might not have come to exercise the power we are considering; no one can say; but

[1] This duty and power of the courts took the place of a proposal in the Convention of 1787 to give Congress the right to declare state laws void, and this proposal was plainly borrowed from the power of the king in council to annul or veto colonial statutes.

the *conscious* line of approach, the conscious course of reasoning was on the basis of fundamental law, natural justice, and judicial independence, while the exigencies of Revolutionary argument developed and fostered the principles in American constitutional law.

CONTROL OVER EXECUTIVE

I have left to the end the statement of the institutional fact which I barely mentioned at the beginning of this paper—the independent power of the court to call executive officers before them and to hold them responsible for their torts. There is no more fundamental principle of American constitutional law than this. Even if it had no actual or constructive connection with the power of the courts to refuse to recognize legislative acts as valid, it is a very striking illustration of the way in which a cardinal principle of law and justice is worked into our institutions. There is nothing in the verbiage of our early constitutions providing for such authority in the courts or for the amenability of administrative officers to judicial authority. It is an emanation from historical antecedents and from English law. But this responsibility of executive officers is in my mind very closely connected with the proposition that legislative bodies are not the final and exclusive judges of what their capacity and authority are.[1] The power of the court to maintain individual right and to preserve constitutional system by refusing to recognize legislative encroachment on individual right must, in the abstract, be connected logically and (if I may so express myself again) psychologically with the power of the court, in proper cases, to refuse to recognize as valid executive construction of executive power and responsibility; I mean, of course, in cases which involve individual right and not involving a political question or administrative discretion. And I do not mean to imply that the courts can control the President himself by directly bringing him before the tribunal.

[1] See the reference to the fact in *Caton* vs. *Commonwealth*, a case quoted *ante*, p. 42. Anyone solicitous to know how the courts have come to exercise this power and announce this principle, if he is unwilling to go back of the express conscious intention of the framers of the Constitution, will be apt to find himself in some trouble and confusion. Whence came the constitutional principle that a legislature cannot delegate its authority? The constitutions do not say so. Whence comes the principle I have just mentioned, the responsibility of administrative officers for illegal acts? Whence comes the acceptance and application of the whole body of private international law in our interstate system?

CONCLUSION

In seeking for the historical background of judicial authority in America I have found it necessary to emphasize a series of fundamental principles which entered into the warp and woof of Revolutionary thinking. As I have said more than once, I am not attempting to make out that each one of these principles, or all of them, demand, by absolute logical necessity, the exercise of the power of the courts to refuse to be bound by legislative enactment. My contention only is that such were the antecedents and that some of these notions or principles were of surpassing influence in the minds of the men of Revolutionary days. The chiefest among the principles I have given are these: first and foremost, the separation of powers of government and the independence of the judiciary, which led courts to believe that they were not bound in their interpretation of the constitution by the decisions of a collateral branch of the government; second, the prevalent and deeply cherished conviction that governments must be checked and limited in order that individual liberty might be protected and property preserved; third, that there was a fundamental law in all free states and that freedom and God-given right depended on the maintenance and preservation of that law, an idea of the supremest significance to the men of those days; fourth, the firm belief in the existence of natural rights superior to all governmental authority, and in the principles of natural justice constituting legal limitations upon governmental activity, a notion that was widely spread and devoutly believed in by the young lawyers and statesmen of the Revolutionary days who were to become the judges of the courts and the lawyers that made the arguments; fifth, the belief that, as a principle of English law, the courts would consider that an act of Parliament contrary to natural justice or reason was void and pass it into disuse, a belief which was especially confirmed by the reference to Coke. Back of all of these ideas was a long course of English constitutional development in which judges had played a significant part in constitutional controversy. In English history courts had held an influential if not an absolutely independent position; Parliament itself had long played the rôle of a tribunal declaring existing law rather than that of a legislative body making new law. The principle of legislative sovereignty as a possession of Parliament was, on the other hand, a comparatively modern thing.

To one at all familiar with the long course of human effort and to the long series of political, theological, and philosophical discussion running through centuries of European history, the assertion of independent judicial power to maintain the fundamental law and to preserve individual liberty, even against the encroachment of legislative bodies, appears to be the natural product of the ages, finding place and opportunity for expression in a new and free country where people were making their institutions—making them, in part, consciously under the guidance of legal and philosophical precept, in part under the influence of great social and historical forces. No one can understand the rise of judicial authority unless he understands the nature and course of Revolutionary argument, the American inheritance of principles of individual right, and the seriousness with which men, in the midst of political turmoil, went back to fundamental principles of political philosophy and strove to make them actual.

II. THE SIGNIFICANCE OF POLITICAL PARTIES

THE SIGNIFICANCE OF POLITICAL PARTIES[1]

In some ways what we call the party management, or the machine, appears to have existed in America before the party. "This day," wrote John Adams in his journal in February, 1763, "learned that the caucus club meets, at certain times, in the garret of Tom Daws, the Adjutant of the Boston Regiment. He has a large house, and he has a movable partition in the garret which he takes down, and the whole club meets in one room. There they smoke tobacco till you cannot see from one end of the garret to the other. There they drink flip, I suppose, and there they choose a moderator who puts questions to vote regularly; and selectmen, assessors, collectors, fire-wards, and representatives, are regularly chosen before they are chosen in the town." In other words, the town-meeting of Boston, with its vaunted freedom of will and frank discussion, only registered the decision of an exterior government. Sam Adams, attending the caucus, scribbling for the newspapers, appealing in shrewd and

[1] This paper appeared in the *Atlantic Monthly*, February, 1908.

simple fashion to the artisans and watermen of Boston, was the primitive boss who brought things to pass. The father of the American Revolution was the leader of the machine.

Although the framers of our federal Constitution must have had experience with scheming caucuses and with wise political managers, they had no conception of parties in any broad sense. Of intrigue, of faction, of enmity between rich and poor, of tendencies in old-fashioned government, of human ambition, they had knowledge in abundance; but of parties organized, officered, drilled, manipulated, fitted to work consistently for power with inconsistent principles, they knew next to nothing. This was natural, for colonial history had not taught them the lesson, though the colonists had had long controversies and had even made occasional combinations. England had not yet achieved systematic party government, but was giving an example of confusion, out of which in the course of the next few years were to arise clear-cut party systems and managements. With infinite pains the men who framed our Constitution laid down ideas of individual freedom; they devised with great cunning a clever system of checks and balances in order that the government might do no harm; but they left to haphazard arrangements, or to voluntary associations unknown to the law and unknown to the theory of the state, the difficult task that was in itself the great problem of democracy. To these associations, which soon arose, was left the task of furnishing a medium for transmitting the will of the people to the government—this balanced mechanism which the Fathers had so nicely fashioned.

Here was the great political and constitutional problem of the decades to come; and clearly enough, if we omit the tremendous struggle over slavery and secession, the development of these associations is the greatest fact in our constitutional history. Little by little these formless voluntary associations were hardened into institutions. They were for a long time altogether extra-legal; only within the last few years have statutes distinctly recognized the existence of parties and made regulations for nominations, with an acceptance of the fact that parties and party mechanism are established and have their important function in the conduct of the body politic. Until about twenty years ago, even ballots were printed by the party officials; the candidates or the political managers were themselves responsible for a large part of the expense of conducting an election. The party organization was allowed to grow undisturbed, and to develop its own capacity for representing or controlling the popular will and for controlling the government described on a piece of parchment locked in a safe at Washington.[1] These party systems themselves came to have constitutions and tens of thousands of zealous officials, whose great object was, not to transmit the unsullied will of the people to the government at Washington, but to advance the interests of their own organizations.

No one doubts the importance of the little group of party leaders in England who by virtue of their inherent capacity rise to the head of the loose party organization and in the Cabinet determine the policies of the government. No one doubts that the English Cabinet is an institution, though it is unknown to the law, and though its conferences are as secret as those of the Vatican. But we have not seen,

[1] It is an interesting fact that this aspect of our constitutional history has received little attention in our histories. A few scholarly treatises have covered some portions of the subject. The most brilliant of these treatises, and perhaps in some ways also the most mistaken, is written by a foreigner, who has the perspective of posterity but also its opportunities for error: M. Ostrogorski, *Democracy and the Organization of Parties*. See also J. Macy, *Party Organization and Machinery*; H. J. Ford, *Rise and Growth of American Politics*.

or are just beginning to see, in America, that the complicated system which manages parties and directs government in this country is an institution to be taken seriously as an established fact, and that the problem of self-government now is the problem of controlling this institution that manages the government which is described by the parchment at Washington. Much of the confusion in our discussion of political problems, much of the incoherence of popular effort, comes from the failure to look facts fairly in the face and to watch the makeup, the methods, and the purposes of the government that has for its purposes the management of what we call the government. The present task of democracy is not to prevent the party management from getting possession of the government, but to make that management responsive to the will of the people. This task is as dignified, as important, and as difficult as the old struggles for representative government, for a responsible ministry, for, in fact, any of the devices and arrangements which were worked out in the course of the long effort to reach political liberty. England, by the revolutions of the seventeenth century, established the principles of her constitution; but her great victory for real self-government came when the party machine was fully recognized as legitimate and was made, in part at least, subservient; the great event was this establishment of the party management in the Cabinet and the fixing of its responsibility.

In America the situation is confusing because we have so many interacting systems and because the mechanism of the government that is described by the Constitution does not easily lend itself to the management of a single party organization. If the party machine could boldly take possession of the government at Washington and manage it in all its ordinary law-making operations, carrying out secret determinations openly and as of right, then we could see the simple fact. But we have clung stupidly to the worn-out idea that the president should not be a party leader but a representative of the whole people, and that his Cabinet is not a party council but a meeting of administrators. In England the party machine—though the law does not see it—is frankly in possession of the government. In America the national party mechanism is organized outside of the government: its makeup is scarcely known to anyone save the professional; we go upon the humorous supposition that since the party is made up of many people, we really control it. Just at present in national politics the situation is comparatively simple.[1] One party controls both houses of Congress, though between the organization in the Senate, where a small band of veterans is in command, and in the House, where one dominant figure valiantly and frankly leads and directs, there are not infrequent differences of opinion. The same party is in control of the executive offices, and the President makes no bones of the fact that he is the head of the party in whose principles he believes and whose success he thinks helpful to the nation. The national committee is under the influence of the real head of the party, who is also the head of the government. When Mr. Roosevelt in 1904 insisted that he must decide who should lead the national committee, he took a step toward simplification, toward bringing it about that the party should in considerable measure be organized in the government. If now party government and legal government could be made one—perhaps forever an impossible ideal in the complexity of our system—the task of realizing democracy would be lightened or at least made plain; the task would be to

[1] This was written in 1908, before the Republican party had passed through the experiences of insurgency and progressivism. The text, however, may well stand as it was written because the facts illustrate the principle.

direct and influence the party system that is frankly in control of the government, and to do this in such a way that the main body of the people would actually determine what policies should be followed and what men should be put into high office. I need not pretend that, even under such circumstances, even with this one government to be looked after, the task would be easy. It is doubtful if even then democracy would be realized as an actual form of political control; but the work of direction would then be made at least comprehensible.

And yet such a discussion as this is absurdly academic and theoretical. We have a complex system outside of the government with an occasional approach to organization within the limits marked out by the Constitution; and the task of a democracy that craves realization is to manage this superior organization and not to let it get entirely away from popular influence. Everybody knows dimly that corporate wealth in this country is managed by remarkably few men; we have recently been instructed with much rhetoric about the "system," and, though we may not take all the rhetoric seriously, we know that what we fear is the domination either of organized wealth or of organized labor. If the emperors of organized riches could overcome their own internal disorganizing individualism and set to work to control the government, what would be their method? Surely not to send their own lieutenants and their trained legions into the offices, or to grasp themselves the places of trust—if one dare use that good word to describe places of profit; not even to seize themselves upon the offices in the party management, the pretorian guard, which controls the government. In their own way, they would from without manage the government which manages the government.

That this sort of thing has taken place in our cities in a more or less disorganized and incoherent way nobody would deny. If the big concerns, which wish to rule the cities in behalf of their own yawning coffers, were fairly organized and not struggling among themselves, we should have three governments: first, the one described by the charter; second, the one represented by the boss and the party machine; third, the one of wealth and lucre. And of these the last would be—not to be sure the only government reaping profit—but the one whose wishes were finally regarded and which could transform desires into acts and pelf. Under such circumstances, would we still cling to the notion that by occasionally casting pieces of white paper into black ballot-boxes we had self-government, and would we content ourselves with thinking that the government described by the charter was our government? Surely it is clear that the thing we want to do is to control the party government, and not to let it fall into the hands of a third combination, for whose power, when once it is made complete, there is no remedy but revolution. This thought, of course, underlies the objection to corporate contributions to party committees. Our means of controlling and holding in check the party management of the national parties are so inadequate, that we almost hold our breath for fear of the annihilation of popular government, when we think how difficult it would be for us to prevent government by organized wealth if the contest were once on.

A glance at our history will illustrate the difficulty of controlling party management and of making it really subject to the will of the main body of the party. The earliest system of presenting candidates for office was through a caucus of office-holders. The governors of the states were nominated by a caucus of legislators, and candidates for the presidency were put forward by party caucus in Congress. Those persons who, because of social standing or influence, were thought capable of holding office, assumed the duty of telling the people for whom they might cast their ballots—a negation of popular determination. This superimposed system was bound to disappear with the rise of democratic sentiment, with the extension of self-confidence among the people, and with the widening of the suffrage that came as the West developed. In the years after the war of 1812, when the masses of the people were beginning to feel their power distinctly, changes were wrought in the nominating system in the states. First came the "mixed convention," made up in part of office-holders, who received into their number persons who were not office-holders; and soon in some of the states the "pure convention" was in existence—a body of men coming from the various parts of the state for the purpose of selecting the candidates of their party for state office. This was the result of a revolt against the self-assumed authority of the office-holders. It was an effort to make the government more nearly and immediately what it pretended to be, the people's own.

In 1824 the régime of the congressional caucus was overthrown. There was then but one party, and personal rivalries within it were the order of the day. When therefore a rump caucus nominated the palsied Crawford for the presidency, this "regular" nomination was treated with little respect by the supporters of Jackson, Adams, and Clay. This disrespect was in part due to the fact that there was only one national party, for under such conditions the authority of customary mechanism is endangered; but to be understood aright the situation must be seen in connection with the general democratic upheaval which was everywhere apparent, which marked the new rise of popular self-confidence, and which shortly, in the advent of the spoils system, heralded an effort of the people to make the government really their own. The protest against King Caucus must be read in the light of the social temperament of the day; it ushered in the reign of Jacksonian self-satisfied democracy, which meant so much in the political, educational, and intellectual history of America.

As no one of the candidates received a majority of the electoral votes, the election of 1824 was decided by the House, a fact hard to be borne by the protestants against congressional nomination. In the next few years the democratic protest was variously registered: by the total disappearance of the congressional nomination; by the triumphant election of Jackson as the man of the people; by the attack on the office-holders and the installation of the spoils system; and by the holding of national conventions to present candidates for election.

Here came, however, one of those recurring contradictions which show the difficulty of popular government, which apparently prove that mechanism is a necessity, and which on the other hand indicate clearly that a mechanism established to register popular desire tends irresistibly to control it. It is apparently an impossibility to set up a transformer, the purpose of which is to transmute public wishes into governmental action, and to have that device work as an inanimate sensitive mechanism. The invention is used at once for the old end, not to transmit power from the people to the government, but as a means of controlling the people; the power passes through such a mechanism downward to the masses and not from them upward to the government. The convention system, the result of an insurrection against dictation from office-holders, was not long a means for expressing popular wishes. The party management used it freely and deftly; it gave new opportunities for the skill of the professional political mechanic. And we are now seeking to get rid of this device originally established to give greater scope for popular desires; in the various states of the union we are now making attempts to establish systems of popular nomination, because it is believed that we can make the government our own by transferring to the people the right to say for whom they may cast their ballots. In national politics, too, we have come to have little faith in the nominating convention, though at times it is impressively subservient, in spite of the management, to popular demands, expressed in all sorts of unmechanical and unsystematic ways.[1]

But of greater significance than the convention system, which came in Jackson's time as a protest against superimposed control and dictation from office-holders, was the spoils system. This, too, was, in national politics at least, the effect of a protest against an office-holding régime, the result in some measure of the notion that the government was not for any official class but for the people. As a matter of fact, of course, it did not operate to democratize the government; on the contrary it provided a

[1] The nomination of Wilson in 1912 was said, for example, to have been necessitated by popular sentiment. The nomination of Taft has not commonly been so regarded.

means of financing party management; it furnished the sinews of war to party government. The men who occupied their time in manipulation for the purpose of getting and holding office and for managing the government were now furnished by the public with the funds for political warfare and for carrying out their plans of campaign. When once a party is fairly organized, with a selected body of leaders, with lieutenants and subalterns in every nook and corner of the land, it needs funds. No matter how praiseworthy the party principles, continuous activity under expert guidance requires funds; and the spoils system was a device whereby the great governmental system which managed the party was provided with funds from the public treasury; for office was given by party leaders to pay party debts, and, moreover, portions of the official salaries were paid over to the party management to finance its operations. It is worthy of note, too, that under the spoils system persons inducted into office because of their activity as party workers were expected to serve the party and its organized board of direction. When once that idea prevails, the real government is obviously the party organization; the so-called government is the instrument, the conventional grooves through which the system standing without expresses its authority.

There has been a great outcry against the spoils system by many who do not appear to see the simplicity of the whole matter and its pre-eminent rationalness. The establishment of so-called popular government brought parties—parties with principles and parties with hunger. We cannot conceive of the possibility of getting on without them; it is easier to imagine the demolition of any part of our constitutional organization, the submersion of a large part of what the Constitution describes, than to imagine our getting on without political combinations; they are our vital institutions, they abide in the innermost spirit of the people. We cannot live under a scheme in which everyone acts as a disassociated atom; organization is an absolute necessity, and we may thank our stars that our genius for politics, if not for real self-government, has brought about the establishment of two big parties instead of a crowd of factions like those which masquerade as parties in continental Europe. Nothing is a greater proof of American political capacity than this organization of two competing parties to manage a government, and that too a government strikingly ill adapted to the party régime.

If then we are to have parties and if we really desire their presence, if they are an essential part of the great task of democracy, how shall they be financed? Under the spoils system they were financed by the government itself, which gave offices and salaries sometimes to incompetent persons, and sometimes when there were no duties to be performed; for the question was not fitness for the office but capacity as partisans. The party machine was furnished with fuel and lubricant at public expense. Recently it has been proposed that campaign expenses should be paid openly from the state or national treasury. This would be to do only what was done indirectly and amid great protestations of patriotism for half a century or more under the spoils system and is still done to some extent. The spoils system is a method of financing political parties, which are the inevitable companions of so-called popular government. Unless men through the country at large are willing to contribute openly and for legitimate purposes to the party organization, or unless men become suddenly so virtuous and altruistic that they are ready to do party service at their own expense, some legal method of furnishing the party organization with funds must be discovered. We should have little hesitation in preferring the spoils method of financing party management to the secret system, whereby large corporations with special interests to be subserved furnish the funds in exchange for favors. Surely the spoils system, if for no other reason, because of its flagrant publicity, is preferable to the system described by Mr. Platt in his testimony before the insurance investigating committee. Of course managers who are honest and are not in the pay of the corporations do get some recompense personally for arduous party service; they get a mild distinction, they get a sense of power, they get the fun of the game. As good whips in England die in the House of Lords, so here a big party leader like Mr. Hanna may become a king-maker in the Senate. But we are forced also to contemplate a leader of a different kind who slips across the Atlantic to open a racing stable and shake the dust of hurrying America from his feet. What shall be the means of financing the party machine is without exception the greatest question of the hour. Without some proper method, honest party government is extremely difficult and real democracy a hopeless dream.

My main theme is the general organization of national parties and their influence in our history; but one cannot approach completeness in discussing the subject without realizing that private autocrats and local rings of the most corrupt character have often retained their power because of their service to the national mechanism. And one must notice too that, in the course of time, there came various predatory methods, which I have no desire to connect intimately with legitimate party machinery. The support of these rings by open use of the spoils—vulgar, expensive, and dangerous though it be—is probably preferable to the systems that have been largely followed. The practice of direct stealing, whereby Mr. Swartwout, collector at New York, some seventy years ago purloined over a million dollars, has been given up as hopelessly banal and crude. The methods of the Tweed ring, though partly those of common stealing, showed more adroitness and originality; they have recently been followed in some measure in other states and cities, and conspicuously in unimaginative Pennsylvania. But the last refinement is to finance the local rings and irrigate their systems, by subjecting corporations to demands for ransom and by leaving the corporations to recoup themselves by the use of privileges or by opportunity to pile up legitimate wealth without fear of brigandage. At times, on important matters, this system has transferred the government from the machine to the corporation. The licensing of crime by the local ruler who owns the government and can issue immunities is again an interesting fact in the general history of popular government. We shall see all these things more clearly, if, amid our denunciation of their odious criminality, we see their connection with the great public duty of furnishing funds for the party system.

There appear at times evidences of an amusing incapacity to see the actual situation. Strong objections, violent protests are made because a member of the party organization is put into office—because, for example, he is given the opportunity of drawing the salary and holding the title of postmaster. Let us ask the protestants frankly why the political managers should be expected to ask the advice of those who have done nothing to care for the interests of party. So long as we have popular government, we shall have parties; so long as we have parties, we shall have party managers; so long as we have managers, we must expect them to look after their interests and their party's nurture. If anyone wishes to stay outside of the party lines, let him do so and let him make just as big and violent a protest as he can against unfit appointments; by his outcry, he too is serving the state; but let him not be amazed at the temerity of the party manager charged with a public duty—for the management of a party can be called nothing less—in putting into office a wheel-horse of the party, rather than some decorous citizen who leaves to others the responsibility for making quasi-popular government a possibility.

I have spoken of the party as if it were bent on controlling the government for certain ends, and as if for that reason it acquired the offices and financed its operation by the spoils system. As a matter of fact, principles are often, if not commonly, adopted to aid in the acquisition of position. While parties have tendencies, almost a personality, and are occasionally really enthusiastic for principles, the party organization and especially the inner circle of party managers have for their end the acquisition of control and of office. This cannot all be explained on the ground of mere greed for positions and salaries, or by any simple and easy statement of impulse and motive. The statement is just as true of the English parties as of the American; and in England with a change of government—a noteworthy phrase—there is little change among the tenants of the civil service. And yet what do we find in England time and again, indeed with ludicrous repetition? We find a party looking for a principle. We ask ourselves quite seriously what principle must be accepted by the Conservatives to get into office, or what by the Liberals; we find over and over again that the party in power has accepted the principles of its opponents and has begun to put those ideas into operation, not without expressions of indignation from the former advocates of the doctrines, who expected by these means to get into office themselves. Such statements as these appear to be a severe condemnation of the whole party régime, and by most persons they will not be accepted as true. But surely they have much truth in them; and our purpose here is not to indict parties or to praise them but to consider their characters and qualities. What do we mean when we say the Democratic party is looking for an issue? We mean at least—do we not?—that the party has a consistency, a being, quite removed from any body of doctrine or any hope of especial legislation or political accomplishment. It is easier to trace a party by its character than by its principles.

A political party may be truthfully defined—or its content roughly suggested—in some such way as this: it is a body of men, somewhat fluctuating in personnel and in numbers, who have begun to work together to attain some political purpose or to oppose other men to whom for some reason they have felt antagonistic. This body, acquiring organization, and gradually developing *esprit du corps* and a sense of self, continues in existence even after its first purpose is accomplished or abandoned, indeed after it has lost a dominating purpose of any kind; it accepts new doctrines to wrest office from its opponents; its activities rest largely on tradition, on party name, on personal pride, and sometimes on a dominating principle. We should not be far wrong if we should declare that there are two or more great armies in existence, each controlled by a select few whose main ambition is victory, and that objects of the people's desire are attained by the organization's accepting a principle as a means of winning success. This does not mean that party leaders have no sincerity. It does mean that they have their full share of human nature, and that a party government would usually throw over a principle which it believed was unpopular and likely to bring disaster. If this is not true, why condemn Mr. Bryan for adhering to free silver when its advocacy had not brought success?

While principles are being hopefully advocated, most party leaders enthusiastically believe in them. This is a beneficent provision of Providence; because human nature is thus constituted, we get such self-government as we do have—a government, organized to get office and to manage government, absorbs popular principles and fights valiantly for their realization. This is also why a party must have a principle; for though it may live without a principle for years, it loses its usefulness, and finds its enlisted men, little by little, deserting. The history of the Whig party is thus explained; for years largely a party of opposition, living for some decades in incoherence and feeding on opportunism, it failed at a critical juncture to accept principles for which the people were beginning to ask organized championship; it "swallowed candidates and spat upon the platform"; it tried to exist by crying out against its opponents and by relying too long on the vague social and economic sympathies which had been its foundation and support.

We need not believe that a party without principles is necessarily unprincipled; it is for the moment unfortunate, not vicious—of course I am not speaking of any local machine that is organized merely for public plunder. We may be sure that leaders are anxiously scanning the horizon hoping for a breeze to fill their sails. But does not this mean that a party is not a body of men united for the purpose of carrying out a principle? Is it not plain that a party is a body of men who act together more or less coherently under discipline of party government and who accept a principle to win success? I am fully aware of the permanence of the tariff issue of the Republican party. No doubt the leaders believe in it and perhaps they would not throw it aside to win the election; but anyone who thinks that the Republican party and the Republican organization do not exist outside of any principles has not thought very much of the significance of political phenomena. Above all, we should recognize that men are born into parties, and that the system exists as a social phenomenon, and that partisan compactness is due to the operation of forces in society and in human nature far beyond the advisability of mere doctrine.

This coherence of the elements of a party, even without reference to principles, has altered our constitutional system. We have on the face of the Constitution a republic made up of republics, each one of which is supposed to be interested in its own affairs and to manage them as it likes; and with these republics is a central government whose operations are confined to caring for a limited number of general interests. But although the Fathers sought to establish a *federal* state, they did establish *national* parties—a strange contradiction, for the tendency of these organizations from that day to this has been to transform the federal republic into a national republic. From these political associations, spreading over the whole country, reaching out into the remotest hamlet, came the unceasing pressure of the national idea. Today the domination of the national party is nearly complete; there are no state parties which look after state issues and which are distinct from the parties and the policies that are of continental dimensions. In every step taken in ward or township, in every nomination made for local office, there is deference to the interests of the great national organization; local interests are nearly submerged; they are regarded occasionally only as the interests of the wider organization allow them to be. When this system is complete, it means nothing more nor less than the disappearance of local self-government; it means a surrender of the local will and the local interest to a wider and stronger power without.

The force of parties as a nationalizing agency,

and their influence for conservatism, was shown with especial clearness in the decade before the Civil War. How long the nation was held together by the strong ties of party affiliation it would be hard to say; how long, in other words, the fact of party delayed attempted secession. Party allegiance held leaders together, prompted them to deprecate sectional strife, and forced them to accept principles in which they otherwise would not have believed; it was stronger in some ways than fealty to the nation itself. Nearly every other bond was broken before these ties of party allegiance gave way. Even the church organization had in considerable measure disappeared before the Douglas Democrats in the Convention of 1860 refused to go the length demanded by the extreme pro-slavery element of the party. As the break-up of the Whig party eight years before had given the solemn warning, so the cleavage of the Democratic party was the end of the Union. The simple fact is this: if we look at the party as a real institution, as of course it is, we must realize that it was almost the last to yield to forces of disunion and disorganization; and, when it did yield, disunion was a fact. The national party proved the presence of national sentiment; but when once a party like the

Democratic party was fairly organized, it had its own consistency, which remained to show astonishing powers of cohesion after sectional passions were aroused, after the real interests of the elements of the party were divergent.

I have said that under the unceasing pressure of national parties local self-determination has largely disappeared. We have thus become in reality, if we are willing to see actualities and pass by appearances, a national rather than a federal state, because it is the will of the national organization which overrules local impulses. If we look at the situation a little more closely, we shall find that we have become not only a national state but a centralized state. It is easy, when one is trying to be precise and clear, to allow emphasis to become exaggeration, and my readers should be warned therefore that there are modifications to be made to my general assertions; but, when all is said, to what a marked extent are local affairs managed, without violent dictation, by the central authority of the party! The object of the party government is not to seek the will of the people and by diligent obedience do what the people may wish; it is not, above all, to give free play to local whims or fancies. A steady gentle pressure is laid upon the remotest school district of the country, in order that in all parts of the land the interests of the continental system may be first regarded. The central organization is busied in quietly and simply smoothing away local differences, in ironing out difficulties that may set the interests of the locality above the success of the whole. Year by year, power and authority do not pass up along the lines of influence from the road district to the committees at Washington; quite the reverse. The vastly complicated party mechanism is not made to obey or to register the behests of the people; it strives for uniformity; it seeks to put the tariff or free silver above good roads or a new schoolhouse or the personnel of a candidate for local office, if the contention over the new schoolhouse or the local candidate endangers partisan homogeneity.

Again let me say this is not pessimism, or even an attack on the party system or the party machine. The party system must be maintained and the management is a necessity; but the tendency of all organization is toward uniformity; organization, whether it be religious organization, trade organization, or political organization, tends to perpetuate itself, to dominate, and above all to be out of patience with differences, peculiarities, local or personal idiosyncrasies. And this is so because system and individualism, system and local assertion, are inherently antagonistic. As well whistle to the whirlwind as expect that any organization should not respond to the laws of its being.

The disappearance of federalism under the influence of nationalism is most obvious in the election of senators. The popular election of senators, as provided for by the new amendment submitted for adoption (1912), ought to be of value in disentangling state from national politics and policies; we may at least hope that it will in some measure set the state governments free and help in re-establishing federalism. For the trouble to be remedied is not the mere method of election by legislators, who are supposed to be approachable—to employ a euphemism. The trouble, or at least the fact, is that the method of electing senators has subjected state politics and state welfare to the interests of a national party. And here again is humorously plain the failure of the framers of the Constitution to see into the future and to do what they hoped. They constituted the Senate as it is, for many reasons; but the equal representation of the states was the result of a demand from the delegations of the smaller states, who feared that, unless such representation were allowed, they would be overridden by their larger neighbors or entirely absorbed by the national system. The Senate, it was supposed, would safeguard the interests of the states. But the system of election made it impossible for the Senate to stand for retention of the real autonomy of the states. As soon as national parties were fairly organized, there was evident necessity of electing state legislators on national issues; to preserve the interests of the party, every effort had to be made to keep the legislature in line. A voter must subserve the interests of his national party by electing a legislator of that party, because a senator's election was at stake; and in consequence national issues were at once involved in every state election, and supremely so when the legislature was to elect a senator. The voter, filled with enthusiasm for his party, would be ready to cast his ballot for a scamp or to neglect every measure of local interest in order to save the senatorship.

Thus through the ceaseless influence of continental parties, the federal character as distinguished from the national character of the republic tended to disappear. Time and time again a party which had disgraced itself in state management, which was under the influence of a corrupt machine, and which was even acting in neglect of the most obvious interests of the commonwealth, has been retained in power, lest its defeat injure the party at large. One can understand how the citizens of Pennsylvania, out of regard for the tariff, are content with a corrupt party management, and even smilingly consent to pay for a state house and its furnishings several millions more than they cost; one can understand their placid acceptance of villainy when by such acceptance they assure a stand-pat policy on the tariff, if that is what is most dear to them. But one could not understand such subjection of common morals and of local interests, if there were no intimate connection between the tariff and the state house, and if our political system were so arranged that a state, without pressure from a national system and a national issue, could look after its own housekeeping. The simple, unadorned truth is that, because of the stupendous organization of national parties in a so-called federal republic, federalism in its most desirable aspects has largely disappeared, and all local issues are so inextricably connected with national politics and dominated by national issues that the locality can with difficulty freely express itself on its own immediate business.

Someone will say that the people can avoid this subjection of state to national issues, if they so desire; that if the people divide on national party lines in electing aldermen and auditors and constables, it is because they wish to do so. That may be true in a sense. The people of Russia could throw off the power of the czar if they wished to. But my purpose is not to argue or to advocate, but to state facts. To say that the people can cast aside the domination of the national party régime is, however, to disregard the control of a powerful organization, a part of whose strength comes from the very multiplicity of local interests and the commonness of the general interests; to disregard the influence of prejudice and pride and party allegiance; to fail to reckon with the imagination to which national party leaders and party contests strongly appeal; and, above all, not to estimate correctly the force of inertia and the sheer difficulty of maintaining state or local organizations distinct from the national party system; in short, to say that the people can if they wish is not to see the difficulty in the real affairs of the political world of clinging tenaciously to complicated federalism instead of yielding to the simplicity of highly organized nationalism.

The situation in the South whimsically illustrates the general condition, because in that section forces are working in a direction quite opposite to that of which we have just spoken. The people of the South are confronted with a difficult local problem and they fear the intrusion of one of the national parties. To subserve, therefore, their distinct particular desires, they continue to support a national party with whose purposes in general they may have little or no sympathy; or, to put the case more guardedly, such is undoubtedly the course of a good many men. Were it not for the local issue, the people in Georgia and Louisiana would presumably soon be divided into hostile companies on questions which separate the national organizations—if it can be said that national organizations are really divided on questions or principles. The people of Pennsylvania, believing it for their benefit to adhere to the tariff party, subject their local politics and internal polity to an organization which is a cog—the fly-wheel more properly—in the general party mechanism. The people of the South, that they may deal with their own local difficulties, adhere to a party in which many of them at least have no particular interest; at all events they work in a party for many of whose tendencies they have no absorbing affection. Partly because local concerns are pre-eminently significant to them, dwarfing all matters of contention between great organizations, partly because of the force of tradition and the bitter deposit of memory, they vote solidly with a party with whom on the question of tariff, imperialism, money, or corporate influence they, or many of them, have no essential sympathy. The people of Pennsylvania, because of an industrial condition, and from phlegmatic inertia, subject local politics to a corrupt machine. The people of the South, that they may manage their own politics, accept the economic policy of the national party. If the Democratic party should obtain control of the national government and be in power for a considerable period —if I may be allowed a humorous suggestion— if it had general national principles of an industrial significance, and if the Republicans, breaking in on the traditional distrust of the South, could obtain a slight footing in that region, there would then be continuous pressure from the general Democratic organization to induce sturdy partisans to forget local issues and avoid factional struggles, lest the result of a cleavage within the party on some matter of state politics should give standing ground for Republican managers.

Party systems and the natural psychological trend of organization are inevitable. If we wish democratic government, we may possibly discover some scheme for managing the party and for transforming its leaders into servants and for retaining their obedience. That was what was accomplished through centuries of struggle against the kingship and against legal government; the government was made constitutional, and that means that it was controlled and checked by a power without. And perhaps by the accumulation of devices, in the course of time, parties may likewise be made responsive and responsible; we may find a new system of ministerial responsibility within the party. There is evidently an attempt to do this or something like it by recent legislation which strictly describes local party committees, and the time may not be far distant when the boss will be recognized as an official. Many times the boss, without holding any office, has been the real government. What value has mere nomenclature under such conditions?

There is, however, no chance of the disappearance of party and of party machinery. Can we not hope for a surcease of the outcry against party management as if it were something that could be done away with by a fit of anger or the sulks? Every movement to overcome it must itself be organized, and, like a party made up to champion an idea, may live to accept reluctantly new ideas to perpetuate itself. At present our self-government depends on our ability to control the party management, as best we can, and, when it is evil or too dominating, to administer defeat. In Russia they are said to have despotism tempered by assassination. This is the system of government that we have in some of our states. The extent of the enlightenment of the despots depends on their good nature and the extent to which they fear annihilation or temporary deposition. In the restraining effect of a rebellion lies the value of reform movements, the temporary tempests, which are wont to elicit laughter from the experienced because in the course of a year or two the older organization is once again in the saddle. But let us not suppose that rulers laugh at insurrections. Fear of defeat will make even the local kinglet, safely guarded within his own winter palace, at least offer libations to virtue by presenting clean candidates for office. Surely, however, in the course of time we can do better than this; we ought to be able to work out a scheme of internal control that will make insurrections needless. Some time we shall democratize and constitutionalize parties.

III. POLITICAL PARTIES AND POPULAR GOVERNMENT

POLITICAL PARTIES AND POPULAR GOVERNMENT

Soon after the adjournment of the federal Convention someone said to Benjamin Franklin, "Well, Doctor, have you given us a republic or a monarchy?" Franklin replied, "A republic, if you can keep it." The most important series of facts in the life of a democratic state is the effort to be and remain a democratic state. And the most important efforts in the history of the United States are those that have been put forth to secure or perpetuate actual self-government. At the present time we realize more fully than ever before the difficulty of actually governing ourselves. We appreciate how many elements are at work seeking to get control of the government in order that they may manipulate the government for their own purposes, or seeking to establish some kind of authority over and above the people, which is contradictory to the fundamental principles of popular government. If we are to take effective part in this continuing struggle for the maintenance of republican institutions, it is incumbent upon us to study and to understand the machinery with which we have to work and the methods and principles of governmental action.

When the Fathers made our constitutions one hundred and twenty-five to one hundred and thirty years ago, they established governments which were checked and limited. Their highest hope was to make a government which could do no wrong, under which individual liberty would be safe. They prided themselves on clever adjustments, on the adroit system of checks and balances which would keep each part of the government from obtaining undue power. They had in mind rather a government that could not do things than a government that could do things, and naturally there were bound to come great readjustments in our governmental arrangements when the people demanded a government that could act and not simply preserve the peace in the midst of struggle and competition of men. In the forming of these institutions, however, they did not take into consideration the formation of political parties. It is evident they had in mind the possible presence of distinct interests, and especially of the differences between the poor and the rich. But of political parties that were organized to acquire office and to manage the government, parties that had consistency and elements of permanence, the Fathers can have had no comprehension. And yet the ink on the venerable parchments was scarcely dry before political parties came into existence and began to take form and consistency. These parties were not nicely checked and balanced. They had no delicate mechanism calculated to make them impotent; but, on the contrary, as the years went by it was apparent that they had capacity for efficient, alert, active action, with skill for securing what they desired.

The men that made our written instruments of government in the eighteenth century, who, as I have said, were so solicitous for freedom and so desirous of restraining government in behalf of individual right, made no provision for the two tasks which, as we have come to see, are the most difficult problems, and probably will remain the most difficult problems of the democratic state. These two tasks are the choice of men for office and the task of conveying to government the will of the people in such a way that the government may be actually responsive to the desires of the people. Unless the masses of the people of the popular state can actually put into office those whom they desire to see there and can effectually transform their own desires into governmental activity and into legislation, they have at the best only the outward forms of popular government and not its essential realities. But, as I have said, the instruments for accomplishing these two great and essential tasks of popular government were left by the framers of the Constitution and were taken up by voluntary associations altogether unknown to the law. In the course of time these associations developed and themselves hardened into distinct institutions of government. They had their governments, their history, their traditions, their character, their tendencies and inherent qualities. They became great competing institutions, each striving to get possession of the government and to control the government. As a consequence, the struggle for the realization of democracy entered upon a new field. It became necessary to control these great governmental institutions which in their turn controlled the government described by the piece of parchment which we call the Constitution. It sometimes seems as if the whole forces of human nature combated the principle of mass government. Organizations, such as political parties, established with the apparent purpose of carrying out principles of democracy and of obeying the behest of the people, came within a short time, as I have said, to have their own tendencies and to be more regardful of their own success and the prolongation of their own lives than regardful for the interests of the people or desirous of being obedient to the wishes of the people.

The truth is that when once an organization is established for the purpose of carrying out a new set of principles, a new force appears to come into existence—the life force of the organization itself, which appears to become a reality distinct from the purposes for which it was established. Thus the great political parties that were established at the end of the eighteenth century came in large measure to exist for themselves alone, and in some respects to be more vigorous and more thoroughly organized than the government; and, consequently, as I have said, a new problem came into existence—not the problem of controlling the government, but the problem of controlling the government which controls the government.

But, in addition, these great institutions—the political parties—established governments of their own. These governments were supposed to be popular governments. I am speaking now of the so-called machinery of the party which has, of course, gone through many developments and alterations since the earlier days. As soon as these governments were in working order they began to lose their quality as popular governments. In other words, they were not obedient to the wishes of the main body of the party. On the contrary they were dominant, they sought to perpetuate their power and to manage the party as they believed it ought to be managed. The idea that the government of a party is ever mildly subservient to the wishes of the main body of the party is one which is totally unacclimated in American politics. Just as the party itself is eager for its own success and its own perpetuation, so the government of the party is eager for the success of the party and for the perpetuation of its own power.

The establishment of these two institutions, if I may venture to call them two, first, the party itself and, second, the government of the party, as they were developed in the course of American history, illustrates admirably the contradictions in the life of the popular state. Both of these institutions, if I may call them two, became dominant and not obedient. And the greatest task of the American people in an effort to realize self-government is and has been the task of managing these great organizations which are not described by constitutions or laws, but which are nevertheless exceedingly powerful. They are rooted in the prejudices, sympathies, and interests of the people. They are vital and real and not artificial. They came into existence to satisfy an actual and palpable want, and yet over and over again their tendency has been not to be subservient, not to be really democratic, not to be helpful in carrying out the great purposes of self-government, but in themselves to constitute problems and difficulties in the way of democratic realization.

If you were asked today what are the real needs of the American state, what is most necessary if democratic government would be a reality, if the people would actually govern themselves, you would probably not advocate any change in our governmental institutions as described by our constitutions; you would say that the people must hold securely in their own hands the reins of party government; they must find some measure of determining for themselves who shall represent them; they must discover some means of determining for themselves what principles shall be acted upon by the government. Thus it is that the problem of popular government is reduced to the problem of the management of parties and the control of the governments of the parties. The simple and unalloyed truth is this: we need to discover some means of effectually controlling the real government that controls what we call the government; and until we can do that we cannot feel that we have become a popular state.

In order to understand the party it is necessary to know of its origin, its character as shown by its history, and its qualities as disclosed by its actual functions. Probably it will help us to know the party as it is if we remember that, though a real political institution, it is essentially modern. We sometimes speak of parties in the ancient world or in the Middle Ages, but as a matter of fact we have no reason for thinking that the political party, as we know it today, is in essentials like the factious combinations of early centuries. The old party, which was better called a faction than a party, represented a distinct class or element in the community; it strove for personal or class advantage; it struggled to dominate the government and make it its own; its opponents were its enemies; its success was likely to mean the proscription or the banishment of its antagonist. It did not have the systematic organization of the modern party. It did not have like functions. The old-time party, the faction, was in general immutably connected with class interest or was rooted in some old personal and racial antagonism whose bitter hostility was inversely proportioned to its reasonableness. Even as late as Charles II of England, the time from which we are accustomed to date the rise of modern parties, the differing elements in the state were more nearly like the hostile factions of an earlier day than like the parties of the present. In truth, although parties, like all other institutions, have a long historical background, they took on their present character only with the establishment of popular government.

So true is this, that it may not unjustly be said that they were created by the opportunities, the necessities, and the responsibilities of modern democracy; and with every advance of democracy, with every effort at fuller expression of popular will, the party has acquired new force. This would seem like a hopeless contradiction in light of what I have just said concerning the dominating character of party and of party government. It may be an inexplicable paradox; but it contains the truth: the party as distinguished from the faction has worthy functions and reaches its true stature only when the popular will is recognized as the determining factor in the state; but organization, which would be impossible under any form of superimposed and autocratic government, tends, as I have already said, to perpetuate its own life. It presents a new machine to be managed, a new system to be controlled. The facts are simply these: democratic government, as distinguished from mere anarchistic individualism, requires organization; and by its essential inherent qualities, organization tends to be self-perpetuating, dominant, and autocratic.

We are led on to face another troublesome contradiction when we see that parties come into existence to foster and promote principles; for this seems hardly to tally with the fact that in a truly popular state there is little room for vital principles or doctrines sharply dividing the people into distinct bodies. The more nearly the state becomes thoroughly democratic, the less need there would appear to be for parties that embody differing principles and tendencies. For the popular state possesses unity. You cannot imagine a real democracy divided into classes, each with its own desires and its own *esprit du corps;* you might have the form of democracy, you could hardly have its essence and real spirit, in a state composed of castes, cliques, or social factions. In the truly popular state there may be, therefore, differences of opinion; but these are presumably temporary, they are supplanted by new issues with the growth of public opinion and with the appreciation of actual, general, and common interests.

Such abstract assertions as these may appear too vague and philosophical to have bearing on practical problems of everyday politics. But a moment's consideration will lead one to see that they help to explain perplexing conditions in practical political life. We are today, for example, in considerable doubt concerning the course and activity of party action. There are some differences between the sentiments and the tendencies of the extreme right and the extreme left; the most conservative of the Republicans are not in sympathy—let us state the case mildly—with the most radical of the Democrats. Other antitheses might be pointed out; but the truth is that the great body of the people, the masses, are so nearly a unit on the essentials of good government and on the desirable tendency of legislation, that party coherence is in the greatest peril. Were it not for the tremendous force of inherited titles and prejudices, were it not for the immense carrying power of habit, it would be difficult for the two great parties to preserve anything like a solid organization; and, as it is, the difficulty of pointing to distinguishing policies and doctrines taxes the ingenuity of the party leader to the utmost. And thus we see that, while parties are begotten in a state where the desires of the masses are carried into execution, parties as carriers of public opinion appear to be less helpful as the state becomes more unified and more socially democratic. Though we can scarcely conceive of a democracy without parties, though without them we should scarcely know how to move along, the development of unified public sentiment diminishes their usefulness, at least, as I have said, as instruments for the transmission of a particular body of opinion into law. What is the fact today? We rely not on the party principle, manifest, or platform, but on the pressure of public opinion. We have confidence in the influence of common sentiment upon both parties and upon all officers. Public opinion, which is so potent, ignores mere partisan alignment and uses platform pledges chiefly as taunts and goads to spur on the men who have made the promises.

Perhaps I am only saying the same thing in another way when I point to the evident fact that parties tend to become alike in the popular state. To the extent that they are distinct, the state lacks unity in reality or in grasp of its essential needs. The old-time faction struggled for itself; the modern party must, at least ostensibly, struggle for the common good. No party which was once seen to have peculiarly at heart the interests of one element of the community could possibly survive; it would not have the temerity to try to live unless, of course, there were elements conscious of their own peculiar and particular interests. But if there were these distinct self-conscious classes, there could not be the essential qualities of democracy. If the Republican party should openly assert that its tariff policy was principally for the benefit of the manufacturer or the big moneyed interests of the country, it could not long survive—unless we have ceased to have substantial unity and have ceased to cherish the essentials of the popular state. At all events we are now so nearly a democracy in spirit that we will not tolerate palpable special privilege; we have cast that old word privilege, with all the ideas connoted by it, into the limbo of the unspeakably undesirable. Privilege and the spirit of American democracy are still impossible companions.

Nothing is more plain to the student of

history than the tendency of one party to assimilate the principles and the policies of its opponent. It is a common saying in England that the Conservatives get on by carrying out the Radical measures. The cleverness with which the Populists' doctrines of a generation ago have been taken home by the standard parties of the nation is one of the most noticeable features of modern political life. I do not say that this process of absorbing Populistic doctrine has been fully worked out now in the great parties of this country; one of them has rigid elements born of long power which do not easily yield to pressure; but enough has been done to illustrate the general principle. The party gradually adapts itself to public opinion, puts on quite virtuously and without conscious hypocrisy the air of supreme originality, and fights valiantly for the issues which it at one time contemned. That you cannot, therefore, distinguish between parties, need not make you hopelessly pessimistic; it is the consequence of vital democratic sentiment; it betokens the fundamental reality of the popular state.

A consideration of these elementary facts helps us to see the folly of so-called minority or proportional representation. If there be anything out of place in the democratic state it is this pretty plan which was supposed to insure liberty and make for justice. Once the fondling of the closet-philosopher, it has become the pet of the crafty politician. If there were distinct elements in the state, each having its peculiar life and distinct interests, each might, with some show of reason, be given representatives to care for those interests. Such is the principle in the states of Europe that are still divided into classes and where there is no general public opinion, no common consciousness. But in America, as yet—thank fortune—we do not need these theoretical schemes which belie the very existence of community interest and common purpose. The minority, in fact, are always represented; for in the democratic state they cannot be a distinct class, and the tendency of any party is to take up the desires of any considerable portion of the community, if, by doing so, it may gain recruits and not lose adherents proportionately. Of course, this is done hesitatingly and slowly; the party in power especially hesitates to burden itself with new responsibilities; but each political party looks for adherents. One party, moreover, approaches as near as possible the outskirts of the other in order that it may entice the stragglers.

The majority party for the time being—watchful of its own strength—takes up the tenets of the minority, those marginal tenets which are most easily annexed and those which appear most likely to attract recruits.

In one respect the minority which is benefited by an existing régime has more than its proportional share of power through the operation of party necessity. A party responsible for the legislation of the government and for its own success, hesitates or refuses to pass legislation though plainly advantageous to the majority if the legislation antagonizes a small minority of its adherents. This is very evident in any situation like that offered by the tariff or by the pension system.

Despite this tendency of parties to become similar in their policies and tenets, it may be that they have distinguishing characteristics. It may be that from the beginning of our government to the present day each of the two great parties has had peculiar inherent qualities. We might with some confidence attempt to distinguish the Conservative and Liberal parties of England; for on the whole probably their names fairly represent their tendencies. But I am not at all sure of the success of such an attempt in American political history. Which of the two great parties has been conservative and which liberal I will leave you to guess. But in any effort of guessing or of establishing by historical evidence, be assured you will be troubled by a maddening tendency of the party in power to become conservative and to hold the good it has rather than fly to others it knows not of. And you will find any party out of power a party of malcontents, prepared to take up new issues that it may get into office. You will find it enlisting in its ranks the unhappy, the visionary, and the hopeful.

This elemental and instinctive tendency of parties is of vital interest to you and me as students of practical American politics. A party in power is strongly tempted to stand pat. The more powerful the organization, the less easily will it move. This is not because of any peculiar perversity of spirit; it is not due to any vicious reactionary tendency on the part of decrepit leaders. It is first and foremost due to the natural inertia of organization. The same thing is true of an ecclesiastical or any other great social organization. It is due in the second place to a feeling of responsibility as well as of power. It is due in the third place to the fact that the discontented leave the party and naturally flock to the party of opposition.

But there is another element in the case. The party in power tends to become regardful of vested interests; it tends, if you want me to say so, to be mindful of "the interests." Let me make it clear why this is so. It is so because, as I have said, a party that has the power feels the responsibility and dreads innovation. But that is not all. The vested interests, the money elements, gravitate instinctively into the party in power. There is no politics in business. This statement is not pessimism nor is it true only of 1912. Study the history of the Jeffersonian party, of the Jacksonian party, of the Republican party, each one of which started as a radical party, and you'll find that they attracted by their success the elements of property and vested interests.

In all such discussion as this I have no intention of aspersing the possessors of money or fortune. We all know that there are men of fortune who are virtuous and patriotic citizens; and we know, too, that there are moneyed interests that have helped to debauch legislatures. I wish here only to point to the fact, first that there is probably an instinctive tendency in possessors of property to support the party which in office feels responsibility and has power; second, that moneyed interests that peculiarly desire governmental protection or governmental favors support the party that can give them. I am explaining myself thus explicitly because I am quite unwilling that any casual expression of mine should be taken to include all moneyed interests in one mass as if there were no distinction between conscientious and conscienceless capitalists.

A cartoon which appeared in a daily paper the other day was drawn by a man who was conversant either with present politics or with American political history or with both. It pictured a dapper old dame walking with lively and confident step toward the White House; the satchel which she carries in her hand is marked "Miss Democracy." She has plainly seen better days, but she is now hopeful and has the springy step of youth. A rotund gentlemen in the background, whose ample form is intended to represent the big interests, is saying, "Nice looking old woman, that. I wish I knew her better." I am not sure that the well-favored gentleman of property does not now know the nice old lady pretty well; but if she reaches the White House, I am sure he will try to know her better.

All this simply shows us how difficult it is to establish and perpetuate popular government;

and how peculiarly difficult it is to maintain a government intent on serving the masses and sensitive to the needs—the changing and developing needs—of the great body of the people.

It is, I believe, a common belief that parties exist to carry out and establish principles, and that without distinguishing principles they are a useless folly. I am not prepared to say that a party can long exist without a principle. Indeed our history seems to show that a certain body of doctrine is needful. But parties can and do exist for a considerable time without any peculiar doctrines; nothing is much more common than to see a party looking for a principle, seeking what we call an "issue." Here, therefore, is one great use for the party; out of power it looks about for interests and tendencies in the body of the people; it is ready to accept principles which appear profitable and popular. Both parties do this in fact, but the minority party is more eager than the one having the advantage of office and authority. This is the way in which we get such popular government as we do get—not, let it be noticed, by the formation of a new party to champion a new principle or to foster a new interest. Third parties are sometimes formed; but they are likely to be quickly absorbed. If the principles they present are looked on with favor by a large portion of the people, these principles will be taken up by one or the other of the older parties or proved by a short time to be undesirable. Three or four parties can be maintained in the countries of continental Europe. This is because of the class system and the rigidity of interests and the absence of the conscious all-pervading democracy which we know in America.

A party appears to need a principle; but it also needs office. For many reasons it is hard for a party without office long to maintain itself. The whole situation clears itself in our mind if we once conceive of a party as a body of men seeking to get possession of the government, and accepting principles and making fervid protestations of patriotism in order to secure office. This again sounds like mere carping criticism and fault finding. But as a matter of fact, because of the natural tendency of parties to grow together in principle and to reach out for what the great body of the people desires, an election contest often reduces itself or is *elevated* into a claim for office, a claim based on character and capacity for effective administration. Would we have such a lamentable condition of affairs if it were clearly accepted as a fact that the party asks for the suffrages of the people only because it asserts that it is the more trustworthy and competent? What has been the issue between Democrats and Republicans in sundry campaigns in the last forty years? Have not the Republicans asserted that they could better be trusted than their opponents to administer the government wisely and well? Time and again in England the question passed on by the electorate has in reality been whether to trust this leader or the other with the management of the government.

The statement that parties exist to get office will lose some of its apparent cynicism if we fairly consider the functions of the party. Until very recently, be it remembered, practically all of the election machinery was in the hands of the political leaders. The machine had a real duty and responsibility. Charged with self-seeking—and probably justly so charged—the party machine or the organization was burdened with the duty of conducting the election, getting out the vote, distributing literature, providing speakers, watching the ballot-box, in short, doing the hundred and one things that are necessary to enable people to act. Charges of machine methods and even of fraud need not blind us to the fact that these men were acting as public officials. We forget in looking upon men as political leaders that they are because of that fact public officials in reality, and it is a significant and far-reaching fact, the influence of which we cannot yet see, that the state has by recent statutes taken notice of parties and has legalized their organization and distinctly limited or described the duties of their officers.

The function then of a political party, a function of overwhelming importance, is to put men into office and to present their claims for administrative trustworthiness. It follows from this that the duty of a leader is to win a victory. Certain it is that to this end he chiefly functions. Granted that the party is a vital institution with real functions in the state, it is necessary to admit that the party officials are doing public service in seeking to attain office. This putting of men into office is the primary responsibility of efficient democracy.

If the party leaders find themselves confronted by an embarrassing dilemma between the choice or retention of principle on the one hand and the acquisition of office on the other, which alternative will they choose? Again I assert that it is not more than a plain recognition of the functions of a party in a democratic republic to say that it may be the duty of leaders to reject a principle or a policy in order to win votes. We might reach this conclusion from an understanding of the nature of democratic government; it can safely be declared as the natural result of the common duties and functions of the party in ordinary conditions. Not long ago one of the leaders of the Republican party, we are told on newspaper authority, was asked by a body of bankers to support a certain measure of banking reform. He is said to have replied, "I don't care a copper what you bankers want; the people want something else." With him the question was not what was the scientific merit of the proposal. He may have thought that as a statesman in a democracy he must proclaim the doctrine that what the people desire, that they must have, even though it be harmful to their best interests. In reality he was living up to his instincts and—shall I say?—his duty as a party leader to advocate what the people wanted in order that his party might be successful at the polls. It was his duty to win the election, not to thrust upon the people principles which would insure defeat. Here, as in all practical human affairs, it is difficult to be logical and precise in dealing with a matter of morality. It is, one may venture to say, however, not immoral to take principles in order to get office; especially would it not be so if the function of a party were clearly understood by the voters. The social immorality arises from deceit, from dodging of honest responsibility, from misrepresentation, and from false pretenses.

Why will a party object when it sees its own policies taken up by another party and carried forward into laws? If the party were eager to secure the adoption of principles, it ought to be delighted to see those principles conquer. But the truth is that the duty of leaders is to hold office, to maintain the organization, to lead it on to new victory. That is why they are leaders; that is what they are for; and they do not care to see good ammunition fall into the hands of their enemies.

The party has and has had another function in America. It has made for administrative and legislative unity. It has helped to overcome the principles of the separation of the powers of government and make a working system. It has made both houses of Congress a single working body and connected the legislative with the executive. Without some such unification it would have been difficult or impossible to establish responsibility; and without some such co-ordinating and concentrating force as that which comes from party consciousness, it might have proved difficult to manage our system at all. The importance of the co-ordinating and unifying influence of party, in a government like ours, made up of men such as our legislative bodies are composed of, can hardly be overestimated. Imagine a House of Representatives made up of four hundred Congressmen, instead of two competing organizations; and imagine again the complete absence of co-ordination and unity of purpose between executive and legislative, and you'll see something of what party does and has done. That this co-ordination might be obtained otherwise is not of moment; the fact is, it is obtained by party consciousness.

It is probably safe to say that in America the characteristic relationship of parties to government has been this: the party organization has existed outside of the government and from its exterior position has sought to control the government. The party has not been organized in the government, as the English party is organized within the English government. In England there is identity of party leadership with governmental responsibility and power. Our relationship of government to parties is seen in its simplest form in a state where a party boss, holding no public office, possibly not holding office even in the machine of the party, is nevertheless the "organization," and, as recognized boss, not only dominates the party but issues his decrees to the so-called government. This plan works well as long as the governor and the legislature are obedient subjects, recognizing the authority of the extraneous boss. As long as the governor obeys the party "organization" and distributes the patronage with sufficient liberality to satisfy the office-seekers and with sufficient decorum not to shock the public, he is an acceptable official. But it may be that a governor, with unusual courage or with irrepressible individuality, thinks that he has something to say; then there is likely to be trouble. The governor is attacked as a no-party man, as an irresponsible dictator, as an intruder, as a marplot, as a visionary; he is fortunate if he secures by dint of inherent power the following of the masses of his party. We have become (or had become, shall I say?) reconciled to the notion that a governor should not make trouble, but should decorously follow the behests of a power outside the party "organization"—this irresponsible power, which carries on its work in secrecy and seclusion. Isn't that a strange sort of a situation in a democratic country?

Within recent years we have passed into a time of strange confusion; we have had governors—we *have* governors—that are not content with registering the wills of the extraneous, irresponsible, self-constituted "organization." When that happens we seem to be thrown into a perfect whirlpool of conflicting authority; we are tossed about on the waves of partisan commotion. The old-time, simple course of things, in which legislature and governor of the same party, guided by the pressure of the unseen forces without the government, worked smoothly along together—the old-time peace has disappeared and we are vexed with the confusion.

Perhaps the inherent trouble is and has been that presidents and governors have insisted on considering themselves publicly as leaders of the whole people and not as party officials. There appeared to be something below their dignity, something a bit unworthy, in being recognized as the heads of their parties, as the persons whose directions were to be followed by the underlings and subalterns of the party. But another trouble has been that the center of the party mechanism has, especially in recent years, been the man who held the purse, who, because of his relation with interests desiring the passing of legislation or the inhibiting of legislative action, was able to pay the expenses of running the party machine—and mayhap other expenses also. We have become accustomed to the notion that a man outside of the government should from secret sources receive contributions—a pleasing euphemism—enabling him to oil the wheels and furnish the motive power of the party mechanism. We have been more or less reconciled to the idea that this man, styling himself the "organization," should really control the government; but as yet we can scarcely endure the sight of a joining of this power over the purse and over the lubricant with the titulary position of governor or president. If by some device party leadership in the states could be disassociated from money or if we could provide for the legal, open, public, honest receipt and expenditure of money for party purposes, there would be less difficulty—perhaps there would be no difficulty—in putting our party bosses in public office, putting our real governors in gubernatorial chairs and calling them *governors*.

Another reason for the ambiguity and for what is at times the perplexing dualism of

American government—I mean the dualism that results from our having a government that controls what we call the government, I mean the absence of identity between the government of a party and the government that is provided by the Constitution—is this: that the executive is the executive; in other words the principle of separation of the powers has militated against the establishment of this identity. The working harmony of the executive and legislative powers has been more effectually and apparently more easily obtained, either by the exercise of a pressure from without, or by the more or less thorough understanding and close relationship between the government of the party and the legislature. Now as I have intimated, within recent days we find governors that take the initiative, and we have presidents also. They assert party leadership—not without violent protests from party members and party workers, who cry out with one accord that the governor or president is a meddler or usurper—or, if they do not cry out, indulge in mutterings of supreme discontent. It is to be noted that this position of the so-called usurping governor or president, this assumption of leadership, is coupled with an effort to control legislation from the executive office, with an effort to ignore the walls separating the departments of government. Governors with strong wills, and presidents, too, have adopted plans of legislative achievement. The most noteworthy examples are President Taft and Governor Hughes and Governor Wilson. One of the most noticeable things in modern political life was the statement made by Mr. Wilson in 1910 that if chosen governor he intended to consider himself the boss of the Democratic party in New Jersey. Ignoring the old assumption of the isolation of the executive, he proceeded after election, because he was the head of his party, to exercise his authority as head and to use his influence, as well as his authority, as governor to shape legislation.

Now it will be seen that such a situation as that I have spoken of in New Jersey is a perfectly simple one and perfectly intelligible. But we should be sure to notice, first, that it runs counter to the practices in this country and conflicts with our prejudices against the identity of party leadership and titular authority in high executive office; second, that a governor may be able to maintain himself in that position only by virtue of inherent strength of character, supported by a realization of a popular demand for a particular brand of legislation; third, that it will be distinctly difficult to maintain that position without control of the money bags of the party; fourth, that by placing direct legislative responsibility and practically direct power of legislative initiative in the administration, it in *reality* alters our form of government —points in the direction of the cabinet form of government.

It should be remembered that we have had in the past other attempts by executive officers to take distinctly the guidance of their parties, to shape legislation, and to lead them to victory. Cleveland did this with his tariff issue, and I am not sure that the results were happy. It is very hard to lead a party to water and harder still to make it drink; and certain it is that you cannot make it drink simply by virtue of getting the best of it in argument. If by chance the recalcitrant turns out to be either an elephant or a donkey, the force of reasoning seems even less efficacious than usual. Roosevelt tried to be the real leader of his party and of Congress. Again, I cannot say the whole thing was a success, either in establishing him as a leader or in committing his party to his policies. When the smoke of the vessel carrying the irrepressible leader away toward the jungles of Africa was seen to disappear on the horizon a sigh of genuine relief came from the lips of many a politician who prized his own power and party peace. In McKinley's time we had peace, partly because we had war, doubtless, and partly because the President had no evident intention of pressing legislation on the organization of his party or dictating to the king-maker from his own state who sat in the Senate.

Under Mr. Taft we appear to be in a hopeless state of confusion and uncertainty. For this there are doubtless many reasons besides certain more or less futile and awkward attempts at party leadership. When Mr. Taft took the presidential chair he was considered a regular, he was heralded as a dove of peace; he was supposed to bring healing in his wings. He was so strong for party solidarity that he ignored the insurgent Republicans in the distribution of the patronage. Soon, however, he developed a legislative policy; he assumed also that he was under obligations to carry out what he believed to be the pledge of the party and what he held to be good party and public policy. I need not confide in you that he is having trouble. His pet measure was carried through Congress by Democratic and insurgent votes. All is not quiet on the Potomac.

Do not suppose that I am attacking this assumed power of political and legislative leadership by the executive of the nation or the state. On the contrary, as an American citizen, I applaud this effort to establish unity and to concentrate responsibility. As a student of American politics I simply try without prejudice to discover and state the facts. As a student of American political history I cannot be confident that this movement is permanent or that we shall see in our time the establishment of initial legislative authority in the executive office. But let no one suppose that, by decrying the assumption of leadership and authority, one is upholding the essence of the time-honored distinction between departments of government and is maintaining our free institutions. The executive, be it remembered, has at all events, by his power to sign or veto a bill, a share in the legislative power; and let it be remembered also that cohesion, harmony, and even let us say effectiveness in government has in the past been obtained by the pressure of party, and often by the pressure and authority of an extraneous leader who was not given any such authority by the electorate. The notion that the fundamentals of our government are shaken when the power passes to the governor or president, to the person chosen by the people to exercise authority, is of course, nonsense; nothing could be more absurd than the outcry of the extraneous boss who is in deadly fear that the executive will trespass on legislative independence.

The tendency of which I have spoken, the tendency toward the establishment of strong executive leaders who are party leaders, the tendency of the head of the government to feel direct responsibility for the course of legislation and for the securing of needed legislative action, may be only a passing phase. But I am inclined to think the examples of the present are too powerful not to be of lasting moment in the shaping of our institutions.

IV. SOCIAL COMPACT AND CONSTITUTIONAL CONSTRUCTION

SOCIAL COMPACT AND CONSTITUTIONAL CONSTRUCTION

Students of American history or of political philosophy need not be told that in the Revolutionary period men believed that society originated in compact. Our forefathers believed too that the state was formed on agreement and that the king was bound to his subjects by an original contract. To secure the rights of life, liberty, and the pursuit of happiness governments were supposed to have been "instituted among men, deriving their just powers from the consent of the governed." These doctrines were living, actual ideas to the men of one hundred and twenty-five years ago. They found continual expression in the speeches, letters, and public documents of the time.[1] In his speech in the "Parson's Cause" Henry maintained that government was "a conditional

[1] The following is a typical example of the announcements of the theories of the time. "Some citizens used the following language: 'If the king violates his faith to, or compact with, any one part of his empire, he discharges the subjects of that part, of their allegiance to him, dismembers them from his kingdom, and reduces them to a state of nature; so that in such case he ceases to be their king. . . . . And the people are at liberty to form themselves into an independent state.'"—Bradford, *History of Massachusetts*, 333–34 (Boston, 1822).

[constitutional] compact composed of mutual and dependent covenants, the king stipulating protection on the one hand, and the people stipulating obedience and support on the other." In the famous argument on the writs of assistance, when, we are told, the child of independence was born, James Otis "sported upon the subject [of natural rights] with so much wit and humor, that he was no less entertaining than instructive." He asserted "that every man, merely natural, was an independent sovereign, subject to no law, but the law written on his heart, and revealed to him by his maker, in the constitution of his nature, the inspiration of his understanding and his conscience."

Locke was the philosopher of the American Revolution, as he was of the Revolution of 1688.[1] The deposition of James and the principles laid down in defense of the revolt against kingly authority undoubtedly made a very deep impression on the colonial mind, and when irritation waxed strong in America against George III, recourse was naturally had to the

[1] There is abundant evidence of the fact that his *Treatises on Government* were read and studied in the Revolutionary period. His *Human Understanding* was used as a text in some of the colleges, and though this book does not cover the subject of government, the psychology of the work was what I may call the compact psychology.

fundamental doctrines with which history had made Englishmen familiar. The revolt was justified on the ground that the king had encroached on the natural and reserved rights of the colonists, and the final declaration that they were "absolved from all allegiance to the British crown," was based on the belief that the king had broken his contract. Not only the argument, but in some measure the language of Locke is used in the Declaration of Independence.[1]

These assertions are not novel and will, I think, be readily accepted by any student who is acquainted with the material of the Revolutionary period. It has seemed to me, however, that sufficient attention is not commonly paid to the influence and bearing of these basic principles of political philosophy in the period succeeding the Revolution. The foundation doctrines everywhere current during the Revolutionary time were not likely to disappear at once, for on them rested the right of rebellion, through them came independence, upon them

[1] "But if a long train of abuses, prevarications and artifices, all tending the same way, make the design visible to the people," etc.—Locke, *op. cit.*, § 225.

"But when a long train of abuses and usurpations, pursuing invariably the same Object, evinces a design to reduce them under absolute Despotism,"—Declaration of Independence.

was founded national existence. We might be willing to assert, without investigation, that the ideas which men cherished and the philosophy upon which they acted would be sure to affect the thoughts and activities of public men during the early constitutional period and for many years after the establishment of the United States. It is certainly important for us to understand the ideas which men held concerning the nature and origin of the state and society, and to know the foundations upon which they believed government to rest. In the study of any period such knowledge and appreciation are needed, but they are absolute requisites for the understanding of men's words, motives, and acts at a time when governments were in process of construction and new states were forming. If we are to start historically upon the task of constitutional construction, we must necessarily begin by seeking to discover how men used terms, and we must likewise endeavor to appreciate their essential attitude of mind toward government and the essential nature of their thinking on matters of political concern.

It may be advisable to state with some explicitness what may be considered the fundamental notions which were commonly accepted when our national and state constitutions were established. Most of these are doubtless familiar to the reader. I shall not attempt to give a consistent philosophy or to set forth the ideas in more than general terms.[1] The underlying idea was that men originally existed in a state of nature free from restraint. Each man was an individual sovereign and possessed of all rights, though dependent entirely upon his own strength to defend his rights. Society was formed by agreement among men, each individual surrendering a portion of his natural rights and retaining others which were inviolably his. Government and political organization also rested upon agreement. Thus through the conscious action and consent of individuals, permanent institutions were established. Now beneath these ideas of political philosophy was what I may call the metaphysical notion, that unity can be formed by the conscious action of so many isolated beings—unity can be formed by the separate movement of isolated atoms. Akin to this compact idea and necessarily bound up with it was the idea that man could

[1] It is difficult, for example, to describe a state of nature with exactness, because of different theories and ideas. On the whole perhaps it is fair to say that men accepted Hobbes's conception of the perfect lawlessness of the state of nature and coupled it with Locke's notion of compact and the resulting government.

bind himself; obligation grew out of consent, and did not necessarily depend on force, certainly not on a pre-existing force. Law was not necessarily the expression of the will of a pre-existing superior directed toward an inferior, but rested like everything else on the consent or the acquiescence of the individual. Not that any individual could at any time cast off his obligations and recall his acquiescence; on the contrary, real obligations permanent and binding came from original agreement.[1]

It will be seen at once that there is something very familiar in many of these doctrines, even at the present. Some of them have become embodied in legal phrases and in political catchwords. To discover just how far these ideas have been perpetuated in writings on municipal law would be an interesting task; but my present purpose is to consider only constitutional law or rather constitutional history and to note the bearing of such theories on the general question of the nature of the United States and the Constitution. In order

[1] See especially the exceedingly able chapter on "Municipal Law" in James Wilson's *Lectures on Law*, in which in the course of fifty pages he attacks Blackstone's definition of law—as a "rule of civil conduct prescribed by the supreme power of the state.' "The consequence is," says Wilson, after a long discussion, "that if a man cannot bind himself, no human authority can bind him."—*Works*, I, 193 (Andrews' ed.)

that the influence and meaning of these doctrines may be more fully seen, it may be well to phrase the fundamental ideas of modern political philosophy. The supposition that society originated in compact is now discarded and with it the notion that man ever existed in a state of nature possessed of all rights. Society is looked upon as organic, a natural thing, and not the result of intellectual agreement; society is not superimposed on man, but, as Aristotle said, man is by nature [originally] a political being. Government may indeed be said to rest upon the consent of the governed considered as a whole, since government in America is distinctly the creature and agent of the body politic; but man owes obedience to the government and to the will of the body politic, because he is born into society and the state, and is an essential portion of it. The state is an organism, a personality, gifted with a purpose and a will. Bluntschli has carried this so far that he has discovered that while the church is feminine the state is masculine; he is ready to tell us the gender, possibly the sex, of the organism. Law is the expression of the will of the body politic, the superior and all-controlling being; law emanates from a being and is binding because of the force of the controlling entity behind it. Sovereignty is the ultimate will and controlling purpose of the body politic.

To the compact philosophy, then, may be said to belong three ideas which were of influence in our constitutional history: (1) The state is artificial and founded on agreement; (2) Law is not the expression of the will of a superior, but obtains its force from consent; a man can indissolubly bind himself; (3) Sovereignty is divisible. I know full well that many of those who wrote of the compact theory believed in the indivisibility of sovereignty. Hobbes held that the monarch was possessed of all power. And Rousseau—who, however, influenced the American idea very little—believed in a sort of indivisible sovereignty.[1] Even Vattel, who was used much more than Rousseau by the statesmen of the latter part of the last century, seems on the surface of things to teach that sovereignty is indivisible; but as a matter of fact his reasonings and arguments on the general subject under consideration do not bear out the idea of the indivisibility of

[1] As the state and society were conceived by our forefathers, *complete political, absolute and unlimited power inhered neither in the state nor in the government.* "Locke and our own forefathers . . . . start with certain natural legal rights possessed by the citizens as individuals, limit the authority of the sovereign power accordingly, and maintain that any attempt on its part to violate these rights is unlawful."—Lowell, *Essays on Government*, 172.

sovereignty; a consistent part of the compact idea of law was that a body of men could surrender a portion of its right of self-control and could be bound by its voluntary agreement, thus limiting and confining its power of self-determination. But if the reader does not agree with this statement, this at least he will accept, that there is nothing in the character or the fundamentals of the compact philosophy which makes a division of sovereignty unthinkable; and if he examines the writings of our early constitutional period he will find the prevalence of the idea that sovereignty could be divided.[1] The tenets of the organic philosophy are directly opposed to the three ideas I have just mentioned: (1) The state is natural and original, and a natural thing cannot

[1] I do not mean to say that no one asserted the indivisibility of sovereignty. Perhaps it was clearly stated in the speech of Morris in the Philadelphia Convention, *Madison Papers*, May 30. "He contended, that in all communities there must be one supreme power, and one only." Wilson in the Pennsylvania Convention hinted once at the same idea and there are a few other instances.

"Though in a constituted commonwealth standing upon its own basis and acting according to its own nature—that is, acting for the preservation of the community, there can be but one supreme power, which is the legislative . . . . yet the legislative being only a fiduciary power to act for certain ends, there remains still in the people a supreme power to remove or alter the legislative, when they find the legislative act contrary to the trust reposed in them."—Locke, *Two Treatises on Government*, II, § 149.

be the result of intellectual agreement; the only result of agreement is an agreement, not a new unity; (2) Law is the expression of the will of a pre-existing superior; (3) Sovereignty, which is the will and purpose of a being, is necessarily indivisible. Divisibility is simply unthinkable.

When the Constitution of the United States was being made, men did not speak or think in the terms of the organic philosophy. Some of them, it is true, were more or less distinctly conscious of the essential oneness of the American people; some of them believed that the states never had been sovereign; some of them, seeing the fact of nationality, demanded that political organization should be in keeping with this fact. But the organic philosophy was developed in the next century,[1] and like all philosophy it came not from the abstract thinking of the closet-philosopher, but from the actual development of society. While philosophic doctrine may react upon human affairs,

[1] Perhaps I should again, from motives of caution, remind the reader that in the text I am speaking in general terms. Burke, for example, because of the historical character of his thinking, saw that the state and society were products of history and were not the creatures of mere momentary planning and consent by puny individuals. But the general truth is as stated above. The full organic *idea* could not come before the organic *fact* of this century, nor could the philosophy come before Hegel and Kant.

human affairs in the progress of history beget philosophic doctrine. If I am right in the assertion that men thought and spoke in terms of the compact philosophy, it follows that we must necessarily interpret their conscious acts in the light of that philosophy. I do not say that it is entirely unjustifiable to interpret the period from 1760 to 1790 in accordance with the precepts and the principles of the organic idea;[1] but I mean simply to assert that if we seek to follow out *historically* the interpretation of the Constitution or to find out what men thought of it at the beginning, we must get into their attitude of mind and understand their method of thinking.

An examination of the writings of the period seems to demonstrate that men approached the subject in hand—the establishment of a new constitution and government—guided by the ideas of the compact philosophy and, moreover, that they often directly and explicitly likened the Constitution of the United States to a new original constitutional or social compact. No

[1] Such a treatment as that of Burgess, *Political Science and Comparative Constitutional Law*, I, 98–108, for example, and large portions of that of Von Holst, seem to me entirely justifiable. But of course it must be borne in mind that the authors are seeking fundamental principles underlying conscious action. I have discussed this matter at greater length at the end of this article.

one who has studied the primary material will be ready to assert that men consistently and invariably acted upon a single principle, that they were altogether conscious of the nature and import of what was being done, and that they constantly spoke with logical accuracy of the process. Such consistency and philosophic knowledge do not appear in the affairs of statesmen. But as far as one can find a consistent principle, it is this, that by compact of the most solemn and original kind a new political organization and a new indissoluble unit was being reared in America. The compact was sometimes spoken of as a compact between the individuals of America in their most original and primary character; sometimes it was looked on as a compact between groups of individuals, each group surrendering a portion of its self-control and forming a new order or unity just as society itself was constituted. Sometimes the idea was not so distinct an application of the social compact theory, but was coupled with the notion that individuals and groups of individuals could enter into binding and indissoluble relationships by agreement, acquiescence, and consent. A few of the more patent illustrations will help in sustaining the position here taken.

Pelatiah Webster, to whom Madison gives the credit of being one of the very earliest to propose a general convention,[1] issued a pamphlet[2] in 1783 in which the general idea is clearly put forth: "A number of sovereign states uniting into one commonwealth, and appointing a supreme power to manage the affairs of the union, do necessarily and unavoidably part with and transfer over to such supreme power, so much of their own sovereignty, as is necessary to render the ends of the union effectual, otherwise their confederation will be an union without bands of union, like a cask without hoops, that may and probably will fall to pieces as soon as it is put to any exercise which requires strength. In like manner, every member of civil society parts with many of his natural rights, that he may enjoy the rest in greater security under the protection of society."

The debates in the Philadelphia Convention contain references to the exact thought so plainly presented by Webster, and give other evidence of the character of the philosophy

[1] *Madison Papers*, Introduction.

[2] A *Dissertation on the Political Union and Constitution of the United States*. I take my quotation from *American History Leaflets*, No. 28, p. 7. The italics of the original are omitted.

within which men were thinking. James Wilson saw as clearly as anyone the necessity of bringing the new government directly into contact with citizens, and he saw, too, that there must be expression for the national life; but he could not say that the American people, already a unit, fused by facts into one body politic, were using this convention as a means of registering their sovereign will in a constitution which would be law and binding on all parts of the body politic.[1] On the other hand he spoke in terms of the compact philosophy: "Abuses of the power over the individual persons may happen, as well as over the individual states. Federal liberty is to the states what civil liberty is to private individuals; and states are not more unwilling to purchase it, by the necessary concession of their political sovereignty, than the savage is to purchase civil liberty by the surrender of the personal sovereignty which he enjoys in a state of nature."[2]

[1] See A. C. McLaughlin, "James Wilson in the Philadelphia Convention," *Political Science Quarterly*, XII, 18, 19.

[2] *Madison Papers*, II, 824, June 8. Hamilton said that "men are naturally equal, and societies or states when fully independent are also equal. It is as reasonable, and may be as expedient, that states should form Leagues or compacts, and lessen or part with their natural Equality, as that men should form a social compact and in doing so surrender the natural Equality of men."—King's Minutes, King's *Life and Correspondence*, I, 610.

"We have been told that each state being sovereign all are equal. So each man is naturally a sovereign over himself, and all men are therefore naturally equal. Can he retain this equality when he becomes a member of civil government? He cannot. As little can a sovereign state, when it becomes a member of a federal government."[1]

Perhaps the clearest evidence that men were thinking in terms of the compact philosophy is contained in the discussion over the question as to whether the Articles of Confederation were still binding. In regard to this matter there were naturally different views. All had had experience with treaties between sovereign powers; and Madison contended that under such a contract as the Articles of Confederation a breach by one of the parties absolved all. Other speakers, considering the articles as something more than a mere treaty or a naked agreement between independent states, and

[1] *Madison Papers*, II, 835. Madison declared that the fallacy of the reasoning drawn from the equality of sovereign states, in the formation of compacts, lay in confounding "mere treaties . . . . with a compact *by which an authority was created paramount to the parties and making laws for the government of them*."—*Ibid.*, 978. The italics are my own. Here we have the compact philosophy in its pure state: agreement founding an authority superior to the creator of that authority. See remarks of Sherman, *ibid.*, 983. Notice also *ibid.*, 1183.

being governed in their thinking in some measure by the compact philosophy, denied that a breach threw the members at once into a state of nature toward one another. "If we consider the Federal Union," said Madison, "as analogous, not to the social compacts among individual men, but to the Conventions among individual States, What is the doctrine resulting from these Conventions? Clearly, according to the expositors of the law of nations, that a breach of any one article by one party, leaves all other parties at liberty to consider the whole convention as dissolved, unless they choose rather to compel the delinquent party to repair the breach."[1] On the other hand Wilson "could not admit the doctrine that when the colonies became independent of Great Britain they became independent also of each other."[2] Hamilton agreed with Wilson, and, denying that the states "were thrown into a state of nature," denied also of course that the Confederacy could be dissolved by a single infraction of the articles;[3] in other words, the Articles of Confederation were articles of union drawn up by communities which were already bound together in a social relationship. Luther

[1] *Madison Papers*, II, 895.

[2] *Ibid.*, 907.

[3] *Ibid.*, 907.

Martin vehemently contended that under the Articles the states "like individuals were in a state of nature equally sovereign and free," and that although they might give up their sovereignty they had not done so and ought not to do so. "In order to prove that individuals in a state of nature are equally free and independent, he read passages from Locke, Vattel, Lord Somers, Priestley. To prove that the case is the same with states till they surrender their equal sovereignty, he read other passages in Locke and Vattel and also in Rutherford, that the states, being equal, cannot treat or confederate so as to give up an equality of votes, without giving up their liberty."[1] Martin also declared that "to resort to the citizens at large for their sanction to a new government, will be throwing them back into a state of nature; that the dissolution of the State Governments is involved in the nature of the process; that the people have no right to do this, without the consent of those to whom they have delegated their power for State purposes."[2]

In this speech, which was one of the longest

[1] *Ibid.*, 975. It ought to be apparent that to men who thought in this way "accession" did not necessarily imply the correlative right of secession.

[2] *Ibid.*

and ablest of the Convention,[1] Martin adhered with remarkable accuracy to the compact theory of the organization of the state and government. So important is this that I venture to rearrange the material just given and summarize the conclusions. While Hamilton and Wilson, as we have seen, held that the people of America were already united in a sort of social compact—or, at least, that the Declaration of Independence did not throw the states into a state of nature in their relations; and while Madison contented himself with asserting that the Articles were similar to a convention among independent states, Martin disclosed the full meaning of what was contemplated from the viewpoint of the social-compact theory. Concluding that the states were now equal as individuals in a state of nature, and that to give unequal voting power in Congress would be destructive of that equality, and hence of the existing liberty, he also pointed out that to recur not to the state governments but to the people for the adoption of the Constitution and the establishment of the national government would mean that all people would be thrown into a state of nature;

[1] The first portion of it, lasting for three hours, is compressed into two pages of Madison's Minutes.

each person was now in society and had a government to which he was bound by constitutional compact, and, if he established a new government over himself, he took away from the state government and redistributed political authority. This he had no right to do without the consent of the state government.

One more quotation in this connection will be sufficient indication that the idea of the social compact was influencing the minds of the framers of the Constitution in the formation of the new government and the foundation of the new republic. When the Constitution was finally drawn up it was presented to the Congress of the Confederation, accompanied by a letter prepared by the Convention and signed by Washington. This letter declared that the framers had continually in mind the consolidation of the Union; but the framers evidently thought that consolidation could arise out of agreement: "It is obviously impracticable in the federal government of these states, to secure all rights of independent sovereignty to each, and yet provide for the interest and safety of all. Individuals entering into society must give up a share of liberty to secure the rest."[1]

In looking over the debates in the state

[1] Elliot's *Debates*, I, 305.

conventions and the pamphlets and essays written on the question of adoption, we find further evidence of the presence of the social-compact theory and of the compact philosophy. Wilson said in the Pennsylvania Convention: "When a single government is instituted, the individuals of which it is composed surrender to it a part of their natural independence, which they enjoyed before as men. When a confederate republic is instituted, the communities in which it is composed surrender to it a part of their political independence which they formerly enjoyed as states."[1] Exactly the same sort of statement was made and the same illustration used by a number of other men. Dickinson, for example, said, "As in forming a political society, each individual contributes some of his rights, in order that he may, from a *common stock* of rights, derive greater benefits than he could from merely *his own;* so, in forming a confederation, each political society should contribute such a share of their rights, as will, from a *common stock* of these rights, produce the largest quantity of benefits for them."[2] Mr.

[1] Elliot, II, 429. McMaster and Stone, *Pennsylvania and the Federal Constitution*, 227. Wilson's *Works*, I, 539 (Andrews' ed.).

[2] Letters by John Dickinson, in *The Federalist and Other Constitutional Papers*, edited by Scott, 789. See also same argument in letter signed "Farmer" in McMaster and Stone, 533. In spite of the fact that in this latter essay sovereignty is said to consist

Hartley in the Pennsylvania Convention said: "That the rights now possessed by the States will in some degree be abridged by the adoption of the proposed system, has never been denied; but it is only in that degree which is necessary and proper to promote the great purposes of the Union. A portion of our natural rights are given up in order to constitute society; and as it is here, a portion of the rights belonging to the states individually is resigned in order to constitute an efficient confederation."[1] Mr. Barnwell of South Carolina "adverted to the parts of the Constitution which more immediately affected" his state. He declared that "in the compacts which unite men into society, it always is necessary to give up a part of our natural rights to secure the remainder. . . . . Let us, then, apply this to the United States."[2] David Ramsay in an *Address to the Freemen of*

in the "understanding and will of political society," sovereignty is evidently considered divisible and to be divided in the new order proposed by the Constitution (*ibid.*, 534, 539). See also, for the same argument, Letters of Fabius (John Dickinson) in Ford's *Pamphlets on the Constitution*, 176.

[1] McMaster and Stone, 292. The reference in this speech to the union of England and Scotland is significant. Mr. Findlay in objection to the Constitution said. "In the preamble it is said, *We the People* and not *We the States*, which therefore is a compact between individuals entering into society, and not between separate states enjoying independent power, and delegating a portion of that power for their common benefit."—*Ibid.*, 301.

[2] Elliot, IV, 295.

South Carolina uses the same expressions: "In a state of nature, each man is free, and may do what he pleases; but in society every individual must sacrifice a part of his natural rights. . . . . When thirteen persons constitute a family, each should forego everything that is injurious to the other twelve. When several families constitute a parish, or county, each may adopt what regulations it pleases with regard to its domestic affairs, but must be abridged of that liberty in other cases, where the good of the whole is concerned. . . . . When several states combine in one government, the same principles must be observed."[1]

The Massachusetts Convention furnishes us with some interesting material. Ames seems to have spoken in very modern language and to have discarded in some measure the idea of compact; he rejected at least some portions of the ordinary conclusions springing from the compact theory. "I know, sir, that the people talk about the liberty of nature, and assert that we divest ourselves of a portion of it when we enter society. This is a declamation against matter of fact. We cannot live without society. . . . . The liberty of one depends not

[1] Ford's *Pamphlets on the Constitution*, 373. Notice also the exceedingly able characterization of the Constitution by Noah Webster (*ibid.*, 29, 45, 55).

so much on the removal of all restraint from him as on the due restraint upon the liberty of others. Without such restraint there can be no liberty."[1] Rufus King, however, expressed his opinion that the American people were the first to obtain a full and fair representation in making the laws through the social compact.[2] Bowdoin referred to the same clause in Montesquieu to which Wilson made reference in his well-known speech in the Pennsylvania Convention, and, relying upon the analogy of the social compact, said "to balance the powers of all the states, by each giving up a portion of its sovereignty, and thereby better to secure the remainder of it, are among the main objects of a confederacy" (a Confederate Republic).[3] It is certainly significant that, when the Massachusetts Convention finally adopted the Constitution, it gave consent in the following words: "Acknowledging, with grateful hearts, the goodness of the Supreme Ruler of the universe in affording the people of the United States in

[1] Elliot, II, 9. This idea of liberty is not new or essentially modern, however. Cicero said, "Lex fundamentum est libertatis qua fruimur. Legum omnes servi sumus, ut liberi esse possimus." Said Thomas Hooker, "It is the honor and conquest of a man truly wise to be conquered by the truth; and he hath attained the greatest liberty that suffers himself to be led captive thereby."—*The Way of the Churches of New England.*

[2] Elliot, II, 19.

[3] *Ibid.*, 129.

the course of His providence an opportunity, deliberately and peaceably, without fraud or surprise, of entering into an explicit and solemn compact with each other, by assenting to and ratifying a new constitution."[1] New Hampshire seems to have used the same words in the resolution of ratification.[2]

In Hamilton's writings are found many references to the social compact. It is quite evident that he had in mind as a working hypothesis the artificial construction of society and the body politic; and in speaking of the new federal Constitution he, like the others, compared it to an original compact formed by individuals.[3] In the *Federalist* he made use of the following language: "But it is said, that the laws of the Union are to be the *supreme law* of the land. What inference can be drawn from this, or what would they amount to, if they were not to be supreme? It is evident they would amount to nothing. A *law*, by the very meaning of the term, includes supremacy. It is a

[1] Elliot, II, 176. It is worth remembering in this connection that Massachusetts called her own constitution a compact.

[2] Walker, *History of the New Hampshire Convention*, 46.

[3] *Works*, II, 322. See also *ibid.*, 320, 376; VII, 294, 334, 336. As may be seen later in my presentation of this subject, the important fact is not so much that men thought the Constitution a social compact as that they thought of society and the state in general as artificial and based on intellectual consent.

rule which those to whom it is prescribed are bound to observe. This results from every political association. If individuals enter into a state of society, the laws of that society must be the supreme regulator of their conduct. If a number of political societies enter into a larger political society, the laws which the latter may enact, pursuant to the powers intrusted to it by its constitution, must necessarily be supreme over those societies, and the individuals of whom they are composed. It would otherwise be a mere treaty, dependent on the good faith of the parties, and not a government; which is only another word for *political power and supremacy.*"[1]

There are certain remarks of Wilson in the Pennsylvania Convention which seem at first sight to deny the compact origin of the Constitution altogether. But it seems to me that he intended to assert that the Philadelphia Convention was not contracting or forming a contract; that the new order was to spring from the people, not from delegates from the states at Philadelphia; and especially that in America there is no inviolable contract between government and society. He came very near to the

[1] *Federalist*, No. XXXIII. The italics are in the original. See also No. XXII.

conception of the people of the United States as one body politic, as a single creating unit establishing the Constitution. Indeed, that may possibly be the idea he had in mind. But it seems more likely that he was thinking of the people of each state as the real establishing authority and of the relationship that was to exist between the government of the United States and the people: "I have already shown that this system is not a compact or contract; the system itself tells you what it is; it is an ordinance and establishment of the people.[1] . . . . If we go a little further on this subject, I think we see that the doctrine of original compact cannot be supported consistently with the best principles of government. If we admit it, we exclude the idea of amendment because a contract once entered into between the governor and governed becomes obligatory and cannot be altered but by the mutual consent of both parties."[2]

It should be observed that the notion of a binding contract or compact between government and governed, which is here rejected by Wilson, was in very evident conflict with Ameri-

[1] McMaster and Stone, 385. This speech is quoted by Bancroft to prove, apparently, that the Constitution was not considered a mere treaty between independent states.

[2] *Ibid.*, 384–85.

can conditions. It could not well be supposed that any government was possessed of sovereignty or that a constitution formed an inviolable and unalterable contract between a sovereign government and its subjects. And yet there was some difficulty in breaking away even from that portion of the old contract notion. Rousseau of course altogether rejected the notion of a contract between the sovereign people and the government, and the French idea was in this respect much more in harmony with later American conditions than was the idea of the Revolution of 1688, although the American Revolution was fought out on the principle of the English Revolution and in recognition of the idea of a contract between king and people. But in spite of its seeming inapplicability to American institutions, the notion was too firmly rooted not to retain its hold long after the adoption of the Constitution. It appears in arguments and discussions as to the nature of the United States and the character and authority of the central government. Jefferson declared in the Kentucky Resolutions that the Constitution was a compact between states and that each state was an "integral party, its co-states forming, as to itself, the other party." But before the paragraph is finished he seems to argue that a contract exists also between the states and the government. As is well known, Hayne in his speech on the Foote resolutions spoke as if the states were one party to a compact and the United States government the other.[1]

These quotations and references may be sufficient to indicate that men were thinking of the possibility of establishing a new political organization and a new government by agreement and consent. It is clear that something different from a mere convention between sovereign and independent states was contemplated. Thinking as they did in the terms and under the limitations of the compact theory and the compact philosophy, they did not speak of the new state as "original" or "organic" or "natural," or declare that a binding law must

[1] "A State is brought into collision with the United States, in relation to the exercise of unconstitutional powers; who is to decide between them? Sir, it is the common case of difference of opinion between sovereigns as to the true construction of a compact."—Hayne's Reply to Webster, January 27, 1830.

"The common notion," says Madison, "previous to our Revolution had been that the governmental compact was between the governors and the governed, the former stipulating protection, the latter allegiance. So familiar was this view of the subject that it slipped into the speech of Mr. Hayne on Foote's Resolution and produced the prostrating reply from Mr. Webster."—Madison's *Writings*, IV, 296. See the correspondence of Governor Troup of Georgia with President John Quincy Adams.

rest upon the force or will of an organism existing before the law was issued. On the contrary, all states were artificial not natural, superimposed not original; society itself was not natural or original but formed artificially, in time, by the conscious intellectual consent of its framers. Inasmuch as government, political organization, and unity can rest on consent, can be based on the action of thirteen bodies acting in isolation, all that was necessary was to obtain the separate consent of the people of the thirteen states.[1]

[1] No one will seriously maintain that Marshall believed that the United States was only a confederation of sovereign states. But did he believe that it was necessary that the American people should exist as a body politic before the Constitution was adopted in order that the Constitution might be a real constitution and the United States an actual unity? "They [the people] acted upon it, in the only manner in which they can act safely, effectively, and wisely on such a subject, by assembling in convention. It is true, they assembled in their several states—and where else should they have assembled? No political dreamer was ever wild enough to think of breaking down the lines which separate states, and of compounding the people into one common mass. Of consequence, when they act, they act in their states. But the measures they adopt do not, on that account, cease to be the measures of the people themselves, or become the measures of state government."—*McCulloch* vs. *Maryland*, 4 Wheaton 316. It is quite possible that Marshall believed that although the people were geographically separated they were acting as a single body politic which was laying down its will in a supreme law. But it is also possible that he thought of a supreme law resulting from the action of thirteen bodies of people, a law which when adopted was to be the supreme law of the land.

Those who likened the Constitution to a social compact seem to have had two ideas somewhat different in character. Some of them had in mind the combination of each person with every other in the establishment of a new society and body politic; others thought of thirteen bodies of individuals each yielding up a portion of its self-control and thus forming a new unity as men do when organizing a simple state or society. Most of the quotations previously given disclose the latter idea. That bodies or groups of men were thus by agreement forming the United States was the thought of Wilson and Hamilton and Dickinson. But Luther Martin, who reasoned on the basis of the compact theory with inexorable logic, insisted that the individual men were compacting together: "It is, in its very introduction, declared to be a compact between the people of the United States as individuals; and it is to be ratified by the people at large, in their capacity as individuals; all which, it was said, would be quite right and proper, if there were no state governments, if all the people of this continent were in a state of nature, and we were forming one national government for them as individuals; and is nearly the same as was done in most of the states, when they formed their governments over the people who composed them."[1]

It is an interesting fact that these two differing views of the way in which the Constitution was established have survived, although writers do not use the words "compact" or "state of nature," or "sovereignty of the individual man," or like expressions. Sometimes we hear it said that the states entered into the Union each giving up a portion of its sovereignty. This is the idea of Wilson, the idea that bodies or groups of men by compact created "a new one."[2] Sometimes it is said that the people established the Constitution; but the thought seems to be, not that the people as a single body politic was acting, but that each individual contracted with others in establishing a new political organization and

[1] Luther Martin's Letter. Elliot, I, 360. The convention of Massachusetts had the same idea, if we judge by the words of ratification.

[2] "When a single government is instituted, the individuals of which it is composed surrender to it a part of their natural independence which they enjoyed before as men. When a confederate republic is instituted, the communities of which it is composed surrender to it a part of their political independence, which they formerly enjoyed as states."—Elliot, II, 429; McMaster and Stone, 227. It does not seem, however, that Wilson was always consistent in his advocacy of this idea. See his opinion in the case of *Chisholm* vs. *Georgia*, quoted later.

recognizing a new government.[1] This is the idea of Luther Martin.

The first important constitutional case before the Supreme Court turned in large measure on the nature of the Union. The opinions of Wilson and Jay are significant, and it may indeed be said that Jay's opinion furnished the basis on which the judicial interpretation of the Constitution has in large measure rested. Wilson declared that there was only one place where the word sovereign might have been used with propriety; the people "might have announced themselves '*sovereign*' people of the *United States*." And yet he goes on to say: "The only reason, I believe, why a freeman is bound by human laws, is, that he binds himself. . . . . If one freeman, an original sovereign, may do this, why may not an aggregate of freemen, a collection of original sovereigns, do this like-

[1] "It is a compact among the *people* for the purpose of government, and not a compact between states. It begins in the name of the people and not of the states."—Letters of Agrippa, Ford's *Essays*, 112.

The survival of the compact method of thought is interestingly shown in Bryce. "The acceptance of the constitution of 1789 made the American people a nation." "The power vested in each state . . . . belonged to the State before it entered the Union." "The loosely confederated States of North America united themselves into a nation."—*American Commonwealth*, abridged ed., pp. 16, 229, 167.

wise?"[1] Jay asserted, with a clearness uncommon even in later decisions, that the people in their collective and national capacity established the Constitution. But he also said in this immediate connection: "Every state constitution is a compact made by and between the citizens of a state to govern themselves in a certain manner; and the Constitution of the United States is likewise a compact made by the people of the United States to govern themselves as to general subjects in a certain manner. By this great compact, however, many prerogatives were transferred to the national government. . . . ."[2] He then reached the conclusion that the "sovereignty of the nation is in the people of the nation and the residuary sovereignty of each state in the people of each state."

[1] *Chisholm* vs. *Georgia*, 2 Dallas 415, 456.

[2] *Ibid.*, 471. For a similar idea as to division of sovereignty resulting from compact, see Pinkney's oft-quoted speech on the Missouri restriction: "The parties gave up a portion of that sovereignty to insure the remainder. As far as they gave it up by the common compact, they have ceased to be sovereign." Benton's *Abridgment*, VI, 439. Monroe said, "In the institution of the Government of the United States by the citizens of every State a compact was formed between the whole American people which has the same force and partakes of all the qualities to the extent of its powers as a compact between the citizens of a State in the formation of their own constitution."—Message, May 4, 1822; Richardson, *Messages and Papers*, II, 147, 148.

In the light of the material which I have cited, one might perhaps be fully justified in affirming that the framers of the Constitution considered it a compact analogous to a social compact, and similar in its origin to the state constitutions in all essential particulars. I think that such is the reasonable conclusion. But whether that be the proper generalization or not, it seems perfectly safe to assert that the student who is interpreting the words and acts of men of the last century must remember the contract theory and the philosophy of Locke. It is well also to remember that men who were thinking in terms of the compact philosophy could believe in the establishment of a permanent and indissoluble body politic as the result of agreement between hitherto separate bodies; that they could believe in the permanent binding effect of a law which had its origin in consent. To them the correlative of "accession" was not secession, but a continuing relationship.

The Virginia and Kentucky Resolutions, if approached from the viewpoint of the compact philosophy, may bear an interpretation quite different from that commonly given them, and different from that assigned to them by Hayne and Calhoun, who had begun to speak in the terms of organic philosophy. In other words, the Virginia Resolutions, at least, can bear just the interpretation which Madison insisted, thirty years after their appearance, was the correct one, because in 1830 he was still speaking as a disciple of Locke and as a statesman of the eighteenth century. If sovereignty is indivisible—as it must necessarily be in the organic conception of the state—then if Kentucky is sovereign, it is wholly self-determinant. But if sovereignty is divisible, the assertion that Kentucky is sovereign is not incompatible with the idea that the United States is also possessed of sovereignty. If a body politic, a state, cannot originate in agreement, then to call the Constitution a compact, and to say that "each state acceded as a state and is an integral party"[1] is equivalent to saying that the Constitution is a mere treaty and the United States merely a league. But if a body politic, a new indissoluble whole, can be established by agreement, between hitherto separate units, if government rests on consent, if a solemn compact is the surest foundation of a state, then to say that the Constitution is a "compact to which the States are parties," is not a declaration that the United States is not a unit or a state. If law is the expression of the will of a pre-existing

[1] First Series, Kentucky Resolutions.

superior body, and if the Constitution is an agreement between equals, then it can in no true sense be law. But if the only way in which a man can be bound is by binding himself, if law springs from consent and agreement among equals, if government itself rests on consent, then the Constitution may have been a compact and nevertheless be law.

The Virginia Resolutions, though based on the principles of the social compact, are not entirely explicit. They may have asserted no more than the right of the states, the parties of the compact, to protest; but they probably meant more. Evidently combating the notion that the central government was the final and exclusive judge of the extent of its own authority, the resolutions declare that the states must maintain "within their respective limits the authorities, rights and liberties appertaining to them." There thus arose the old problem of the legal order under a government resting on compact or consent; who was to judge whether the compact had been violated? If the people were to judge, was this not the same as mere wanton anarchy or confusion? Locke faced the question in his famous Second Essay: "Who shall be the judge whether the prince or legislative act contrary to their trust? . . . .

To this I reply, The people shall be judge. . . . . If a controversy arise betwixt a prince and some of the people in a matter where the law is silent or doubtful, and the thing be of great consequence, I should think the proper umpire in such a case should be the people."[1] This of course is something entirely different from the right of each man to judge and to refuse to be bound by a command he believes to be beyond the power of the prince under the compact. Locke also declares for majority rule: "For, when any number of men have, by the consent of every individual, made a community, they have thereby made that community one body. . . . . And thus every man . . . . puts himself under an obligation to every one of that society to submit to the determination of the majority and be determined by it."[2]

If Madison meant to assert that the meaning of the compact should be decided by the majority of the states, his doctrine was in essence that of Locke just given: if he meant—as probably he did not—that each state should individually judge, his doctrine is not essentially different from that of Jefferson and the Kentucky Resolutions which I shall discuss in the

[1] Second Essay, §§ 24, 242.

[2] *Ibid.*, §§ 96, 97.

next paragraph. This idea, that those that made the compact must judge, came out even in Calhoun's theories, although as we shall see Calhoun did not at all consider the Constitution a social compact, and did not think, to use Locke's phrase, that a number of men by the consent of every individual could make a community. Partly because he desired to prevent the disorganization, implied by complete state sovereignty, and partly because he wished to maintain the idea that there was something less than palpable interstate anarchy based on mere state caprice, he provided in his scheme for a convention of the states, in spite of the fact that, in accordance with his theories of sovereignty, even three-fourths of the states could not bind the individual protesting state, which must retain the right to pass upon the constitution and to leave the Union; it was not obliged to submit to the majority.

Jefferson's resolutions more thoroughly present the social-compact notion than do Madison's. Suppose the Constitution is a sort of compact, analogous to the social compact, made up of parties—in this case, states—hitherto in a state of nature, and suppose that the government of the new order assumes powers not granted by the compact, or, in other words, not surrendered by the parties to the compact, what is to be done? In meeting this question Jefferson is evidently thinking in terms of the compact theory, and this theory must always be distinguished from that which would look upon the Constitution, or any formal organization, as if it were established by the will of a body of individuals composing one legal or moral person. "Every state," he said, "has a *natural right* in cases not within the compact . . . . to nullify, ... ", etc. These words were stricken out and do not appear in the final draft of the Kentucky Resolutions as they were passed by the legislature. Again he said: "That the co-states recurring to their *natural rights*, in cases not made federal," etc.[1] The whole of these Resolutions is clearly based on the theory that each state a party to the compact had the right and duty to protect its reserved rights, its natural rights, not transmitted to the government set up by the compact. This theory is entirely different from that which would look upon the states as wholly sovereign and possessed of all rights. The states had surrendered a *portion* of their rights;

[1] Italics my own. See Jefferson's *Writings*, Ford ed., VI, 301, 308. The latter of the two quoted clauses appeared in the last clause of the Kentucky Resolutions as adopted.

while each state had given up a portion, it was entitled to protect the portion not surrendered. The argument and the viewpoint are the argument and the viewpoint of the American Revolution, not of the South in the Civil War. The intent was to combat the theory, as the Revolutionists had done, that government was possessed of all power. The Resolutions have commonly been misread because they have been viewed from the standpoint of Calhoun's theory of law and of state sovereignty, not from the standpoint of eighteenth century political-thinking.[1]

If one starts with Madison's philosophical ideas the interpretation which he put on the Virginia Resolutions, when he wrote of them in the period from 1830 to 1835, is the reasonable, logical, and inevitable interpretation. Is it

[1] Madison, in the days of South Carolina's nullification, evidently troubled by Jefferson's use of "nullification," thought that Jefferson meant by nullification "the natural right, which all will admit to be a remedy against insupportable oppression"—in other words the right of revolution (Madison's *Writings* [ed. of 1865], IV, 410). This brings up the whole question of the right of revolution, one of the most puzzling questions in the realm of social compact thinking, and I cannot here discuss it. Evidently, however, Jefferson was arguing against the theory of unlimited power in the national government based on its own final power of interpretation; and he was insisting on the right of each state to protect its reserved rights, just as an individual, entering into the social compact, can defend the rights he has not given up.

proper to approach the resolutions with any other ideas than those held by the writer? It is worth while to quote a few of his words written at this later time: "It has hitherto been understood that the supreme power, that is, the sovereignty of the people of the States, was in its nature divisible, and was, in fact, divided . . . . ; that as the States in their highest sovereign character were competent to surrender the whole sovereignty and form themselves into a consolidated State, so they might surrender a part and retain, as they have done, the other part. . . . . Of late, another doctrine has occurred, which supposes that sovereignty is in its nature indivisible; that the societies denominated States, in forming the constitutional compact of the United States, acted as indivisible sovereignties, and, consequently, that the sovereignty of each remains as absolute and entire as it was then. . . . . In settling the question between these rival claims of power, it is proper to keep in mind that all power in just and free governments is derived from compact."[1]

[1] Madison's *Writings*, IV, 390, 391. See also *ibid.*, 61, 63, 75, 294, 395, 419. How fully the nullification theory rests on the indivisibility of sovereignty is seen by an examination of the address to the people of South Carolina by their delegates in convention.

These words of Madison go, in my opinion, to the root of the matter. Calhoun's proposition rested on the doctrine of the indivisibility of sovereignty, and this was a notion resulting from the fact that he was beginning to think and speak in terms of the organic philosophy.[1] He did not, as far as I can find, in so many words discard the social contract in general until he wrote his *Disquisition on Government*, some sixteen years after the nullification trouble. But as a matter of fact the strength of the argument for complete state sovereignty and the right of secession rests on the philosophic conception of the indivisibility of sovereignty; and coupled with this philosophical conception is the idea that states do not originate in agreement and that law is the expression of the will of a superior being. I do not mean to contend that Calhoun consistently spoke in terms of the organic philosophy. On the contrary, he occasionally fell back into the thought and expression of the preceding generation; that was inevitable. But his argument, as it was developed, really rested on philosophic presuppositions foreign to the thinking of the

[1] Madison, IV, 394, gives a beautiful example of how absolutely impossible it was for the clearest thinkers to adhere at first to the doctrine of indivisible sovereignty of a "moral person." Rowan's speech is in Niles's *Register*, XXXVIII, Supp., 46.

time when the Constitution was adopted.[1] If the student of Calhoun's writings does not agree with me in this, perhaps he will be willing to admit that the argument in behalf of state sovereignty, as it has been developed and worked out, for example by Alexander H. Stephens, relies on presuppositions belonging to the organic philosophy. When once the defender of the position has demonstrated that the states were sovereign before the Constitution was adopted and that they adopted the Constitution as separate states, he is ready to believe his point proved; because he believes that unity cannot spring from agreement, that an agreement between isolated beings ends in agreement and nothing but agreement.

Madison's letters of the nullification period are a complete answer to Hayne and Calhoun, written from the standpoint of the men who made the Constitution. But the same sort of reply came from other sources. Jackson's proclamation, for example, is written on the old lines of the compact idea: "The Constitution of the United States, then, forms a *government*,

[1] The reader may notice especially that in his letter to Governor Hamilton of August, 1832, Calhoun expended great effort to show that there had been no such body politic as the American people before the adoption of the Constitution. The adoption, therefore, he would seem to say, by thirteen bodies politic does not make law but agreement.

not a league; and whether it be formed by compact between the States, or in any other manner, its character is the same. . . . . Because the Union was formed by compact, it is said the parties to that compact may, when they feel themselves aggrieved, depart from it; but it is precisely because it is a compact that they cannot. A compact is an agreement or a binding obligation. It may by its terms have sanction or penalty for its breach or it may not."

Of great interest in this connection are the resolutions which some of the states drafted in answer to South Carolina.[1] They are exceedingly good examples of the continuance of the social-compact idea and of the compact philosophy. Massachusetts spoke as she might have spoken forty years earlier: "The constitution of the United States of America is a solemn Social Compact, by which the people of the said States, in order to form a more perfect union . . . . formed themselves into one body politic."[2] Ohio's answer was much the same: "Resolved that the Federal Union exists in a

[1] It is sometimes overlooked that nearly every state which answered the resolutions of South Carolina declared her theory a heresy and of dangerous tendency. See even the resolutions of North Carolina and Mississippi.

[2] *State Papers on Nullification*, Boston, 1834, 128. The quotations above given are of course only a small part of these replies.

solemn compact, entered into by the voluntary consent of the people of the United States, and of each and every State, and that therefore no State can claim the right to recede therefrom or violate the compact. . . . . "[1] The argument in the report of the Senate committee of Massachusetts is especially significant, because it so clearly and keenly analyzes the position of South Carolina and meets the proposition of the nullifiers so squarely. The committee saw that nullification rested on this assumption: "The States were independent of each other at the time when they formed the Constitution; therefore they are independent of each other now." To one thinking rigidly in the terms of the organic philosophy the assumption that the states were independent and separate when they formed constitutions is equivalent to a declaration that they were independent afterward or at least that the mere adoption of the Constitution did not deprive them of independence. But the Massachusetts committee answered in terms of the compact philosophy, and thus stood in the position of the men of 1787, who could see no reason why an actual unity should not result from consent. "The rights and obligations," said this committee,

[1] *Ibid.*, 206. See also p. 214.

"of the parties to a contract are determined by its nature and terms, and not by their condition previously to its conclusion."[1]

Generalizations with regard to this subject are dangerous and difficult; but it certainly seems inevitable that one must draw at least this conclusion—Men differed, in part at least, because of their different fundamental conceptions, and those conceptions were philosophic. One side declared that the Constitution was a compact and therefore not binding; the other side declared that the Constitution was a compact and therefore was binding. One side said that sovereignty was indivisible; the other declared that it was divisible and had been divided. The organic philosophy is accepted by modern philosophic publicists and writers of political science. Will they say that, because the men of 1787 did not act and speak in the terms of the philosophy which arose from the civilization of the next century, a philosophy which was first decisively manifested

[1] *Ibid.*, 119. "Now there can be no doubt, that independent states are morally as capable of forming themselves into a body politic, as independent individuals. . . . . Hence, were it even admitted, that the states were distinct and independent communities at the time when they framed the Constitution, the fact would no more prove that they are distinct and independent communities now, than the fact that two parties to a marriage contract were single before its conclusion goes to prove that they are single afterward."—*Ibid.*

in Hegel and given full expression by the more modern political philosophers, they did not do what they intended to do? Would it not be as wise to insist that, inasmuch as Locke's philosophy is now rejected, James II was not overthrown, and that his descendants are entitled to exercise the prerogatives of the British crown? The judicial construction of the Constitution has remained in large measure in accord with the compact philosophy. Shall we declare that judges and lawyers must abandon the traditional idea of the division of sovereignty or the theory that the states come into the Union surrendering a portion of their sovereignty, and that the acceptance of the Constitution made the American people a nation? Is there not much to be said in favor of adherence to old and original notions?

But the organic philosophy of course obtained its followers among those who gave the national construction to the Constitution, and before the Civil War men were meeting the advocates of secession on their own ground.[1] The organic

[1] I have omitted reference to Webster, because Webster's speeches on the subject require longer and fuller exposition than I can give them in this article. Story, too, deserves special examination; but, as was to be expected in his time, there is great confusion in his writings and a single idea is not carried through logically. He sometimes talks in terms of compact; sometimes not.

character of the United States can be sustained on an interpretation of acts, facts, and forces of the Revolutionary period, 1760–90, which takes into account the realities which underlay all seeming conditions or the conscious acts of men. I do not mean to affirm or deny that men were clearly conscious of national life and of the idea that the states were not truly sovereign.[1] I mean simply to say that by the very character of the organic philosophy one is compelled to go beneath the surface and to see realities. Of course men, who argued from the basis of the organic idea and nevertheless maintained that the United States was more than a multiple of units organically separate, did not in so many words declare that they had taken up new philosophic ground; but in fact they had left compact thinking behind them and from the new viewpoint met the declaration of state sovereignty with a new interpretation of history which naturally and logically sprang from the

[1] I have already shown that some men believed that the states were not made independent of each other by declaring independence from Great Britain. See the speech of Pinckney before the South Carolina Convention, as well as many assertions in the Philadelphia Convention, or Hamilton's well-known statement that a nation without a national government was an awful spectacle. They were more or less conscious of the reality—the existence of national life.

new methods of thought. The ordinary mode adopted was to deny that the states were ever sovereign and to insist, as Lincoln did, that the Union was older than the states.

An excellent example of this method of interpreting history is found in Alexander Johnston's article on state sovereignty in Lalor's *Cyclopaedia*. Granted that sovereignty is not simply law-making power, but the will, the impulse, the controlling motive of a mass of people organically fused together, where are we to find such a will, where are we to find such actual fusion, this dominating reality, before 1789? Evidently not in the incompetent states, for to call them sovereign is to give a meaning to sovereignty incompatible with the organic philosophy: "The states declared themselves sovereign over and over again; but calling themselves sovereign did not make them so. It is necessary that a state should be sovereign, not that it should call itself so, while still sheltering itself under a real national authority. The nation was made by events and by the acts of the national people, not by empty words or by the will of sovereign states. . . . . The national feeling held the nation together, and forced the unwilling state governments to stand sponsor to a new national assembly. Such was the convention of 1787."[1]

Now my contention is that this philosophic interpretation of facts, seizing the underlying verity, is not only admissible but necessary for those who insist on reading the events of those days from the viewpoint of the organic philosophy. But I also contend that if the *conscious* deeds and words of men are to form the sole basis of our argument, then we are thinking as becomes those who are bound by the conceptions of the compact philosophy, the distinguishing characteristic of which was that it never went below the consciousness in whatever field of human thinking it showed itself, in the two centuries during which it reigned supreme; and we are also bound to remember that the framers were thinking and speaking in terms of compact and believed that agreement could establish unity.

That methods of constitutional interpretation as well as arguments on the essential character of the United States should be influenced by the development of political philosophy was inevitable. For philosophy is only one field of thought, unless it be, as the philosophers claim, the sum of all. The politi-

[1] Lalor's *Cyclopaedia*, III, 791.

cal philosophy of this century is merely the systematization of ideas and modes of thought produced by the developments of the century. And it is exceedingly significant that the organic idea should have first been used in behalf of a declaration that the United States was not organic and that it should have found expression in the acts of a state where society was and had been from the beginning peculiarly unitary in its makeup, in the acts of a state which had from early days felt its individuality. It is a striking paradox that the organic philosophy should have formed the basis for the defense of slavery which was disorganizing the nation. Paradoxical, too, is the fact that abolitionism received its being from the growing realization that all men were one, from the prevalence of the humanitarian spirit which has found verbal formulation in the precepts of the organic philosopher.

When organic thinking has shown itself in all fields of thought—in science where men have ceased to speak of the isolated creation of matured species, or even of the isolated development of a single animal, but speak rather of the organic character not simply of an isolated specimen but of the natural world; in history, where the investigator looks behind the conscious acts of men to the hidden forces which were working in society, and smiles at the idea that Caesar overthrew the Republic or that Lincoln destroyed slavery; in sociology, where students give themselves up to the study of social change and social regeneration; in metaphysics, where the scholar seeks to show the unity, which exists in all seeming diversity, and can explain nothing except in its relations and as part of a whole—when all the forces of modern life have drawn men together and made society more truly and really one than ever before, save, perhaps in the little states of ancient Greece, it is perfectly inevitable that an organic notion of political society should prevail. It was inevitable, too, that political thinking and argument in the course of this century should have been materially affected by the modification and development of society. The constitutional history of the United States is in no small degree taken up with tracing opinion and assertion as to the actual character of the Union; and the historian is compelled to notice the change which took place in the opinions, words, and thoughts of statesmen as they were influenced by the change in society and by the prevalence or growth of doctrines as to the origin and nature of the state. The Civil War was doubtless caused by economic conditions, and by economic and moral differences; but each of the contending parties was struggling for what it believed to be the law. Opinion as to what was the law depended on the interpretation of history and also upon the acceptance or rejection of certain philosophic conceptions.

My purpose in this paper has been to show: (1) that the men of one hundred and twenty-five years ago thought within the limits of the compact philosophy; (2) that they carried the compact idea so far that they actually spoke of the Constitution as a social compact; (3) that it is necessary for us to remember their fundamental ideas and to interpret their words and conscious acts in the light of their methods of thought; (4) that in the development of modern organic philosophy new ideas were introduced and new meanings assigned to terms; (5) that from this latter fact, from the inability to agree on fundamental conceptions, arose confusion; (6) that the doctrine of state sovereignty as it has been developed rests on philosophic presuppositions almost if not entirely unknown to the framers of the Constitution; (7) that if we use the terms and insist on the ideas of the organic philosophy, we are entitled to seek the realities lying behind the words of men.[1]

[1] The argument for state sovereignty rests on two main pillars. One we may call historical statement; the other is metaphysical. The historical statement rests on an interpretation of facts in a way characteristic of compact thinking, i.e., it is superficial, not seeking realities back of appearances or mere conscious acts. The metaphysical suppositions are organic—or non-compact:

STATE SOVEREIGNTY

I	II
a) The states were separate, 1776–88.	*a*) The action of separate entities cannot make unity.
b) They adopted the Constitution as separate entities.	*b*) Law rests on will, on power, not on consent or agreement.
	c) Sovereignty is indivisible.

Strike out either one of these pillars and the main argument for state sovereignty falls.

V. A WRITTEN CONSTITUTION IN SOME OF ITS HISTORICAL ASPECTS

A WRITTEN CONSTITUTION IN SOME OF ITS HISTORICAL ASPECTS[1]

That an institution of government, like an institution or practice of society, is a growth and not a creation is now an accepted proposition. No one seeks to argue for it; no one endeavors to deny it. The introduction of this idea into our political thinking strongly influenced our methods and our ideas. In no field of study has the evolutionary idea shown itself more strongly than among workers in history and political science. And yet occasionally one is surprised by seeing how recently this idea has manifested itself in the examination of some historical problems. Until a short time ago, the Constitution of the United States was commonly spoken of as if it was created by some two score men who debated and wrangled in the old state house at Philadelphia during the anxious and trying summer of 1787. Of course it is true that all things are new; and the federal Constitution was in one sense a new product of the past. But the

[1] An address delivered at the celebration of the fiftieth anniversary of the adoption of the Constitution of Iowa, March 19, 1907.

historian sees its fullest meaning only when he studies the long period during which the fundamental ideas and the master principles of the instrument were being worked out. The idea that the Constitution was not in great measure made at Philadelphia was first successfully attacked only about twenty years ago, when scholars began to show how large a portion of its contents was borrowed from state constitutions, which were themselves the heirs of colonial practices.

But this notion that at given moments, at trying crises, inspired geniuses arise to fashion wondrous entities out of preceding nothingness has played in all our affairs a conspicuous rôle. The American people, who but yesterday were a European people, casting aside the trammels of old-world life, and breaking their way into the new atmosphere of an untried continent, forced to shift for themselves and to adapt themselves to strange conditions, believed actually that they were sufficient in their strength at any moment to create what they needed or desired. This absence of historical perspective was perfectly natural, and there was something inspiring in the enthusiasm and assurance with which problems were solved, or at least valiantly attacked. Possibly this easy self-confidence was quite as useful and much more effective than would have been any serious contemplation, any sober reflection over the forces, the successes, and blunders of the past. And yet the readiness to go ahead blindly in answer to the promptings of the moment is not the characteristic of the wisest statesmanship; it is not the nature of the freest state; for the highest freedom must come from right thinking; the best statesmanship must come from self-knowledge—a knowledge of the real state of which the statesman and lawmaker is himself a part, a knowledge to be gained by a study of the state's growth and not simply from the little space of one's own forgetful experience.

This introduction is not, I think, inappropriate on an occasion when we celebrate the founding of a constitution which has lasted half a century. We are pausing here to look back for fifty years, to do honor to the men who were instrumental in bringing into existence the fundamental law of this great state, to realize that under that law a people has grown in numbers, in strength, and in prosperity, and to be thankful for the wisdom of the statesmen who wrought so wisely and so well. But we need not think that the constitution of Iowa was made here fifty years ago, or that we can understand its significance, if we limit our view to the debates of the convention, the decisions of the courts, or the prosperity of the people. This constitution, like all others, has a long and interesting history, reaching far back of the days when these men met here. Some of its provisions can be clearly known, only if we follow their courses through centuries.

ORIGIN OF AMERICAN CONSTITUTIONS

Students of American constitutional history begin at least with the charters that were issued at the end of the fifteenth century. In fact the colonies that sprang from feudal beginnings, like Maryland or Pennsylvania, demand for their understanding a knowledge of feudal principalities; Maryland takes us back to the time of William of Normandy, if not eleven hundred years to the time of Charles the Great. A colony like Massachusetts, founded as a corporation, calls for an understanding of the early trading companies of half a millenium ago. And thus we see that the modern state constitutions have an honorable lineage; instead of being struck off in a moment of inspiration to suit an emergency or a temporary exigency, they are the products of effort and struggle and experience; they are molded and fashioned by the needs of passing generations. Such a thought as this doubtless makes us hesitant about recasting our laws and makes us skeptical of our ability lightly to create what the moment seems to demand. But the development also shows us that man cannot consciously create unchanging institutions for the future; that history, social forces and needs are the real makers. And after all there is no great need of unreasoning fear; you cannot cut yourselves off from the past; it is here with you and will meet you as a friend or an enemy at every turning of your career.

It is not my intention to dwell at length on the development of state constitutions from the old corporation charters. The examples of Connecticut, Rhode Island, and Massachusetts are there where everyone may read. It is interesting, to be sure, to trace the development of the Massachusetts constitution from the charter, or articles of incorporation, of a company—the president or governor of the company became the governor of a commonwealth; the assistants (the board of directors as we might call them) became the council or senate; the freemen of the company (the stockholders, to use a modern term) became, by representation, the deputies, or later the house of representatives. It is profitable to trace the growth of Maryland from a palatinate modeled on the palatinate of Durham into a self-governing state, gradually shaping its institutions to meet the wants of a free people who were growing in capacity for self-government under the stimulus of new opportunity. And of course we must remember that these new western states were, in many ways, but replicas of the eastern states, and that these new communities owe their constitutions therefore to the long history of aspiring colonists and to the shaping and upbuilding work that went on through a century and more of colonial history.

There are, however, other aspects of the subject upon which I wish to dwell; only by studying these can we see the full significance of the modern written state constitution. I have intimated that the history of these documents can be traced back to the feudatories of the Middle Ages or along another line back to the trading charters of the same era. But following another line, a line of fundamental ideas, we find again that we need to go some distance to the past to appreciate what we have.

COMPACT AND NATURAL RIGHTS

It has been said that the modern idea of popular sovereignty, of democratic control, took its rise with the little groups of Separatists, who in the time of Elizabeth set up their right to come together and worship as they chose. Each little band of worshipers considered itself a church, capable of deciding for itself the principles of its action and establishing its own polity. It is true that any method of historical investigation, which attributes a wide and influential movement vitally affecting a great portion of mankind to one particular episode or to one group of men who can be isolated and numbered, has its elements of untruth; but the connection between the movement for self-determination in church and the movement for self-determination in politics is fairly evident. As to form and methods at least this connection is clear. The assertion that men could govern their own ecclesiastical affairs was a revolt against the principle of superiority in the affairs of the world, a revolt which made way for the assertion of popular control in political affairs. I am not now insisting on the value of the Reformation, which many would consider a misfortune. I am not now emphasizing the individualism that is significant of the Reformation and to which many would attribute the growth of personal freedom. I am confining my attention to this movement for ecclesiastical self-government in England.

We know very well that it was a little body of these Separatists that founded Plymouth and there set up their self-governing church and self-governing state. The famous Compact, of which we have heard so much, has been both unwisely praised and unwisely depreciated. Upon it the little Pilgrim state was founded; for, whatever we may say of technical law and of the subordination to England, Plymouth was to all intents and purposes self-governing and was reared on this Compact, which was a church covenant in fact, turned to new uses to form the basis of a state. It was but the first of a series of plantation covenants; for, while the constitution of Massachusetts was forming, growing out of the charter of a corporation, here and there men were organizing little self-governing communities, built upon the notion of individual right to do what one would with oneself and on the notion that one could form a community by agreement with others. We have not in our histories sufficiently marked the significance of these plantation covenants. We have treated the compact political philosophy of Milton and Sidney and Locke, and other great writers of the seventeenth century, as if they were writing in the rarified air of abstractions and vague theory, and as if the compact origin of society and the state were but a convenient fiction or a useful fancy, forgetting how it in essence underlay the doctrine of Independency and was carried into effect in the churches of the Separatists, forgetting, too, that in the wilds of the new world little groups of men were giving examples of common life and political control.

At a time when men were actually living up to the notion that people were separate and could organize a body by agreement, it is not to be wondered at that the philosophers and political writers should set up political theories based on the notion that society was organized by the action of detached individuals, by abstract individuals, so to speak, who came together to surrender a part of their self-control in order to preserve the rest. Not that I mean to declare that the philosophers actually borrowed their ideas solely from the towns of New England, or even, perhaps, from the Independents of old England; for the doctrine of compact and of a natural right that antedated society was much older than New England or than Cromwell's soldiers. The contention is, first, that this philosophy is more concrete and appears as a more natural emanation of its time, if we connect it with the actual deeds of men; and, second, that Independents were doing in England in ecclesiastical matters the very things which the Puritan philosopher was claiming to be the natural order and process of things in the social and political world. Anyone interested in the political as well as the philosophical influence of Independency will find food for contemplation in the fact that in the efforts at constitution-making during the period of the Great Rebellion of England, in the arguments for establishing a state without a king, the soldiers and officers of Cromwell's army, the Independents, very evidently insisted upon a basis of right and a basis of action quite in advance of that set up by the lawyers and statesmen of the same party, who had not broken away from the old ideas of law and custom and were not ready to start with individual separation and to announce the right to organize a state and a government on the basis of the agreement of the people.

Probably we have not given sufficient weight to the influence of New England on Old England in the days of the Great Rebellion. To measure influence is beyond the skill of the historian;

but we are justified in believing that the reaction of the New World on the Old was even then considerable. We are justified in believing that the Puritans of England knew of the success of the men who came across the water to found a Bible commonwealth, and it seems reasonable to believe that the example even of such a state as Rhode Island, distracted and incoherent as it seemed to the orthodox men of Boston, must have had considerable influence with the debaters and thinkers of the trying years, when men were struggling with a tremendously difficult thought—how could a state rid itself of a king, and how could a popular government resting on the consent of the governed be actually brought into existence?[1]

[1] No one having any conception of the part played by covenant in the theology of at east some of the advanced Protestant sects could very well fail to see the connection between the whole theological notion and the conception of the organization and powers of the state. Not only did churches, the Congregational churches, have covenants, but the very existence and perpetuity of the world rests, according to this notion, on covenant and agreement. It is the covenants of God, the pledges by which he binds himself, upon which we rest and upon which we base our hopes and faith. The assurance that the Great Sovereign is bound to his people by solemn covenant and will not disregard his obligation is thus the basis of Christian hope. Covenant, agreement, and promise formed the serious central thought of stability, strength, and fulfilment. In this way, as well as in many others, the essential notions of Protestant theology worked their way into the conception of the character and obligation of the state.

It was inevitable that the men, who were seeking a new political order in the middle of the seventeenth century, should have trouble in seeing their way with clearness along lines that appear to us now fairly obvious. That government sprang originally from the people was proclaimed as a self-evident truth. "It being manifest," as Milton says, "that the power of kings and magistrates is nothing else but what is only derivative, transferred, and committed to them in trust from the people to the common good of them all." But how a new government was actually to be brought into existence was another question, a government derived from the people and obtaining its powers from the people. Devoid of practical machinery and experience, the advanced thinkers of England proposed to act upon theory and to establish a government on the expressed consent and agreement of individuals, as if each were detached and could enter by his signature into a new compact and establish a new government over himself. Nothing is more suggestive to the student of American political institutions than the proposals and the arguments of the men of the Great Rebellion in England, when they were confronted with the task of organizing a commonwealth, of carrying out their philosophic ideas and of really rearing a state on the consent of the governed.

It is full of interest to American students because one hundred and twenty-five years later a like task faced the men of the Revolution, who sought argument for denying the asserted control of Parliament and for throwing off the rule of a king who by "a long train of abuses and usurpations" had "evinced a design to reduce them under absolute despotism." The argument and philosophy of the American uprising against George III take us back at least to the Great Rebellion and to Cromwell's Ironsides and disclose the essential truth in the assertion, that in the American Revolution the England of the seventeenth century met and maintained itself against the England of the eighteenth.[2] No sententious utterance like this is wholly comprehensive and sound; but it brings out the great fact that the principle that threatened the divine right of kings and asserted the divine right of the people,

[2] See for one illustration of the likeness of the two revolution movements the following: "That when a person trusted with a limited power to rule according to lawe and by his trust (with expresse covenant and oath also) obliged to preserve and protect the Rights and Liberties of the people . . . . shall flye to the way of force upon his trusting people, and attempt by it to uphold and establish himself in that absolute tyranical power so assumed over them, and in the exercise thereof at pleasure; such a person

and that proclaimed that government was derivative and kingship a trust, found its refuge in America in the seventeenth century, developed there in quietness in the spirit and capacity of the people, and came forth to challenge the power of England in its Stamp Acts and Port-Bills, and to be used as the basis for proclaiming that these united colonies are and of right ought to be free and independent states.

I wish this statement to be taken not merely as an attempt at rhetoric, but as sober historical truth. The philosophy and the argument, the basis of assertion of the American Revolution, are a striking reproduction of that of the great rebellion in England. The interesting historical fact is that the declaration of the philosopher and the soldier and the Separatist pamphleteer of the middle of the seventeenth century formed the argument for the successful revolution of the eighteenth; and their descendants on this side of the water carried those ideas into effect,

in so doing, does forfeit all that trust and power he had, and (absolving the people from the Bonds of covenant and peace betwixt him and them) does set them free to take their best advantage, and (if he fall within their power) to proceed in judgement against him, even for that alone if there were no more."—A Remonstrance of His Excellency Thomas, Lord Fairfax and of the General Council of Officers, London, 1648, pp. 21, 22. Compare this with the thought of the Declaration of Independence.

not simply by throwing off the power of George III, but by embodying the ideas in institutions and by reducing them from abstract formulae to actual practical governmental principles.[1] As far as theory was concerned, the men of 1650 had worked out fully the basis of the American Revolution.

The notion of natural right, of the origin of government in agreement and consent, did not find its sole expression in the manifesto of independence or in the oratory of the statesman and the demagogue. America, taught by experience with popular institutions, proceeded, sometimes with misgiving and doubt and at other times with haste and overconfidence, to work out the methods for establishing governments on the free consent of the people. The statesmen of the time might have actually treated each individual as if he were wholly abstracted from society and ready once again to enter into a new social order out of a state of nature in which he was a detached and separate individual; for such indeed, as in 1650, was the theory underlying much of the thinking of the

[1] The student of the Revolutionary period knows that many lines of argument were followed. I have in mind here the salient and impressive argument that came from Massachusetts and to some extent from other colonies, from Jefferson as well as from Samuel Adams.

time and underlying the constitutions that were to be framed; but the leaders did not totally disregard established institutions, draw up a contract, and call for signatures. In some of the states the methods were illogical; in Massachusetts, under the guidance of John Adams, a new constitution was framed on the logic of the principles of the Revolution. The constitution of Massachusetts, drawn up by a body of delegates especially chosen for the task, was discussed and debated in the town-meetings and ratified by their votes. In that state there came clearly forth the functions, the place, and the character of the constitutional convention —one of the greatest contributions, perhaps the greatest contribution, of America to politics and political order—a method of establishing a commonwealth without confusion, a method of permitting the people to rear, as Adams said, "the whole building with their own hands," a method of making actual the dreams of philosophers, political pamphleteers, and statesmen of the seventeenth century in England.

Again, let us not lose ourselves in words; this identical problem had been attacked by Puritans, from whom the early men of Massachusetts came. The significance of what the Americans did in developing the constitutional convention can be seen in its simplicity and force, only when seen with this background of discussion, uncertainty, and desire that fully showed themselves in England one hundred and thirty years before Massachusetts was called on to form her constitution. It may be that, had the principle of contract been strictly lived up to, no one would have been bound by the Massachusetts constitution unless he voted to ratify it; but doubtless any malcontent would have been free to leave the new commonwealth; and we must not lose sight of the fact that the constitution purported on its face to be a social compact.[1]

INDIVIDUALISM IN MODERN LAW

The principle that the constitution is a compact into which each individual enters out of a state of isolation, which the philosophers called the state of nature, has deeply and perhaps permanently affected our public law. It is astonishing and impressive to see the modern jurist talking in terms of compact and natural

[1] "We therefore, the people of Massachusetts, acknowledging, with grateful hearts, the goodness of the Great Legislator of the universe, in affording us in the course of His providence an opportunity, deliberately and peaceably, without fraud, violence or surprise, of entering into an original, explicit and solemn compact with each other, ... do agree," etc.—Preamble of the Constitution of Massachusetts.

rights, after the fundamental conceptions, on which those terms rest, have altogether disappeared from ordinary modern thought and modern life. We know perfectly well that government rests on authority, not on the consent of separate individuals; that that authority is the people of the state as an organized political unit; that the constitution expresses the will of that unit, which is known to the law and exists in fact as an entity to establish the constitution. We know, too, that there never was a state of nature in which men existed as monads and from which they entered into society. We know that rights in any legal sense are the creation of law and exist because of government, and that all the new needs and the new justice are not implanted in the heart of primeval man, but have come as he has grown and as society has developed in depth and complexity. We see that the whole thinking, upon which the notion of natural rights and of compact rests, deserves the word artificial; it includes the notion that men consciously, out of stuff in their own hands, can deliberately make a society or a state, as a cabinet-maker would fashion a bureau or an easy chair. We know that every branch of modern scientific thought is governed by the thought of growth, of unfolding, and not of conscious creation. We thus find perpetrated in our constitutional law—not to speak of other branches of jurisprudence—a method of thinking that the rest of society has entirely abandoned; and one of the greatest puzzles of modern times is to adapt a system of judicature founded in extreme philosophic individualism to the needs of a society which in some of its aspects is almost burdened with its capacity for expressing the truth of organic growth and organic being.[1]

Perhaps it would be more nearly correct to say that there is always in society a conflict between the individual and society; but, with all our aggressive individual initiative, the Americans have been gifted too with humanitarian sentiment and with remarkable power of political and social combination. The great combines are in themselves made possible by this spirit and this capacity; and it is a striking fact that, manifesting as they do this phase of American ability, and illustrating in all their

[1] I do not mean to lose sight of what appears to be an historical fact and therefore not artificial, that from time immemorial there seems to have been in England a sense or a feeling, if not properly expressed in law, that there were "real restrictions" upon king and Parliament, a certain continuance through the centuries, of the old individualistic feeling of the Teutonic people. Cf. Jellinek, *The Declaration of the Rights of Man and of Citizens*, 93, Farrand trans.

activities the essential organic compactness of American life, they seek to be governed by the principles of pure individualistic law, inherited from a time of individualistic thought and endeavor. I am not unwilling to admit that the doctrine of natural right and of contract may be a convenient fiction, and I should like to believe that law, based on a principle of thinking foreign to the activity and foreign to the thought of the community in which it acts, can be abiding and useful; but there is an evident difficulty in adjustment. Whatever my fears or beliefs may be, the facts are so; and surely it is a startling truth, that just as a phase of human thought, which in some of its aspects was older than the Christian era, was beginning to pass away from the human mind, new bodies politic should be established in this new world based on these old fundamental conceptions, which were indeed for the first time thus given adequate institutional expression.

The great movement for individualism came to its fullest fruitage in the Revolution, and was installed in instruments of government that were declared to be permanent; states were organized on a basis of individualistic democracy, just as democracy was about to leave its phase of pure individualism and reach out for a higher, deeper, and different meaning—moving on into a condition of society in which the most selfish should reap their highest reward not through individual and detached effort, but through combination; in which the propelling forces that are upbuilding come from surrender to the spirit of brotherhood and from an effort to raise one's fellows; in which, more than ever before, government is called on to do the things we cannot separately do ourselves. We have fully abandoned the idea that the sole duty of government is to keep the peace and to leave to the individual the task of struggling in all kinds of competition with his environment and his neighbors. We do not believe, as Tom Paine says, that government, like dress, is a badge of lost innocence. We have left far behind in most of our thinking the notion that government is man's enemy. The old democratic ideal of man free from restraint, rising by virtue of his own buoyancy to the place he earns by dint of his unaided effort, has not, we hope, entirely gone; subjection or a stagnant condition appears still the essence of injustice. But we are beginning to see that competition, unqualified and unregulated, may be bitterly unjust, and above all that great combinations that take advantage of social organization to work for personal ends need restraint and control in the interest of humanity and society. And so again the puzzling problem which is being worked out in the legislative halls, in the social order, in the books and brains of thinking men, is how to adapt institutions based on individualism, the product of centuries of effort to reach personal right and personal justice free from the restraints and the wrongs of external and arbitrary power—how to adapt such institutions and how to fashion our political thinking to a new order of things. No more significant contrast could be made than that to be drawn between the utterance of the present leader of the party that claims its descent from Thomas Jefferson, and the assertions of Jefferson himself in his famous inaugural of 1801:[1] "Still one thing more, fellow-citizens—a wise and frugal government, which shall restrain men from injuring one another, shall leave them otherwise free to regulate their own pursuits of industry and improvement, and shall not take from the mouth of labor the bread it has earned. This is the sum of good government,

[1] I need not say that this contrast is simply an historical fact and not intended as an indorsement or refutation of the advanced democratic collectivism which now dominates one wing of the Democratic party of the day.

and this is necessary to close the circle of our felicities."

GOVERNMENT BOUND BY LAW

To understand properly the modern written constitution and the problems of its existence, we need to look at another line of development. The efforts of English history were to establish a government of laws and not of men—to discover some method of avoiding arbitrary government. Of course this effort was directed against the king, and, in considerable measure because of this opposition to the king, the commons of Parliament developed their powers and their privileges. But in the seventeenth century this effort reached a wider stage, and, though at various times we see a desire to increase the powers of Parliament against the king, and though often in fact this desire appears to be controlling, it is plain that the ablest minds went farther and sought a government bound in all its parts by some power greater than itself and checked by some restraint which it could not sweep aside. One needs to read only the instrument of government of 1653, in light of the discussions that preceded it, to see that it was a faint approach to a realization of this idea; and the same thought appears in

Harrington's *Oceana*, a work which had considerable influence in America one hundred and twenty-five years later.[1]

I have remarked on the trouble men had in thinking of a suitable means of bringing a real popular commonwealth into existence; their difficulty in discovering some suitable manner of binding the government, when once it was created, was even greater. They saw the necessity of stability, of regularity, of rigidity if you will, in the fundamentals of government and in the bounds of its power. Liberty was not even for them, in their individualism, mere opportunity to do what one would; it consisted, in the minds of the best thinkers, in the privilege of living under a government restrained from acting on whim or caprice. But how attain such an end? No government, it was assumed, could rightly disregard the rights of nature; every governor must rule for the common good. "And so," says Locke in his second *Treatise on Government*, "whoever has the legislative

[1] Harrington approached an adequate description of government by the Boss, when he said, "And Government, to define its defects, or according to modern prudence, is an Art whereby some Man or some few Men, subject a City or a Nation, and rule it according to his or their private Interest; which because Laws in such cases are made according to the Interest of a man, or some few families, may be said to be an Empire of Men, and not of Laws."

or supreme power of any commonwealth, is bound to govern by established standing laws, promulgated and known to the people, and not by extemporary decrees, by indifferent and upright judges, who are to decide controversies by those laws."[1] It is not clear that Locke saw those laws as anything more than laws promulgated by the government itself; he did not see—perhaps he did not care to—the use of a constitution superior to government and binding upon it. In the end he resorted to the right of revolution, as a remedy or an assurance that government would keep within limits: "Should either the executive or the legislative, when they have got the power in their hands, design, or go about to enslave or destroy them, the people have no other remedy in this, as in all other cases where they have no judge on earth, but to appeal to Heaven."[2]

It was this principle of the unalterability of standing law that underlay the American

[1] Locke, Second Treatise, § 131. And compare § 22, where he declares "Liberty of man in society is to be under no other legislative power but that established by consent in the commonwealth, nor under dominion of any will, or restraint of any law but what that legislative shall enact according to the trust put in it." Locke, of course, wrote forty years after the Great Rebellion; but he phrased admirably much of the thinking on which the advanced actors of the Commonwealth proceeded.

[2] Locke, *op. cit.*, § 168.

Revolution. The writings of Sam Adams, the Father of the American Revolution, once and again declare this doctrine, maintaining that the English constitution, in its essentials, was not what the Parliament might for the moment declare it, but unchangeable; and this very unchangeableness was the basis of liberty. Helped by their experience of life under a written charter of government, the people of Massachusetts, in their argument against Great Britain, carried forward to a logical conclusion the principles of Harrington, Locke, and Sidney, and the Puritans of a century before. "In all free states," the representatives of Massachusetts declared, "the constitution is fixed; it is from thence that the supreme legislative as well as the supreme executive derives its authority. Neither, then, can break through the fundamental rules of the constitution, without destroying their own foundation."[1] "There are, my Lord, fundamental rules of the constitution which, it is humbly presumed, neither the supreme legislative nor the supreme executive can alter."[2] Thus the Massachusetts representatives in 1768 expressed the idea of a binding constitution and of the source of

[1] Written in 1768. Samuel Adams, *Writings*, I, 170, 171.

[2] *Ibid.*, 156.

governmental authority superior to government—a constitution unalterable because it has its foundation in the immutable laws of nature. Few facts in our constitutional history are more worthy of attention than this meeting of the lines of progress in the announcement of a proposition on which new commonwealths were to be reared and a great war fought to a conclusion: one line runs from the charter of 1628–29, which incorporated a company, a corporation indistinguishable on the surface from the great trading companies like the East India Company or the Hudson Bay Company, whose officers were necessarily limited by the terms of the charter; another line runs from the discussions of the philosophers and soldiers of the seventeenth century in England, who were striving to describe a government of laws and not of men; another line is to be traced to the Separatist foundation of church government, the principle of religious individualism, and the organization of polity in agreement and covenant.

But the Americans went farther than announcement. They fully institutionalized this principle of the unalterability and fixity of the constitution. They drew up constitutions impregnated with the principle that liberty exists where government is limited; and little by little they came to the fulfilment of the idea that government is not the state, that it is the servant of the people, that it acts within specified limits, and, to sum all, that constitutions are themselves laws. As a result, any act purporting to be done by governmental authority is mere usurpation, void, if it goes beyond the limit of law. This proposition, fairly easy for men who had lived under colonial legislatures, strikingly concludes the great development of English constitutional history toward a government of laws and not of men and strikingly answers the anxious questioning of the men of one hundred and forty years before. It rests, of course, upon the idea, now made actual, that the government is not the state, and that the fundamental law springs, not from government, but from a power superior to government, the state itself. In realizing this idea and by making the constitution law, the courts were for the first time in history called in to apply the constitution as law, and to sustain the foundations of the state. From the mere fact that the constitution was law, the courts were under obligations to recognize its binding force.

Although the judges in a few of the individual

states had announced, in some four or five decisions (1780–87), a principle similar to this, the Constitution of the United States was the first document distinctly to announce the fact that it was law. This declaration, moreover, was made pre-eminently to support the arrangement of a federal state, to offer reasonable assurance that the states would not do anything contrary to the Constitution; for it was declared that the Constitution, laws, and treaties should be the supreme law of the land and the judges of every state should be bound thereby—in other words, that the judges of the state in deciding suits must recognize and apply the Constitution of the United States. Only one who has studied the efforts of the thinkers of the seventeenth century to reach an ultimate beyond government, and to make this ultimate of permanent and binding effect, can appreciate the significance of the declaration that the Constitution is law or see the full meaning of this calling in the courts as a third institution of government to maintain and sustain the essential organization of the body politic.

The idea that the Constitution is law and enforceable in courts has occasioned some criticism and dispute. For at certain junctures even those, who were not unwilling to admit that the legislature was bound by the constitution, have asserted that the activity of the courts is an unwarranted intrusion, although it is based simply on the principle that the law emanating from the people is superior to any act contravening it. And there has arisen, on the other hand, the very foolish idea that the supreme court of a commonwealth is the only tribunal capable of disregarding the law of the legislature on the ground that the law is unconstitutional—an idea based on the strange notion, that only the highest tribunal is called upon to declare and apply the law in distributing justice to litigants. It is, moreover, not uncommonly said that the legislature is confined to considering merely the expediency of measures, and that the courts alone can look into their constitutionality; but this is another absolutely illogical proposition—as if the legislators themselves were under no obligations to endeavor to execute the trust of the people and to keep within the bounds of activity marked out by the people in the making of the constitution. But possibly the most illogical and dangerous of the recent doctrines is the declaration that an administrative officer does not render himself personally liable by the enforcement of an unconstitutional law or administrative act.[1] Such a doctrine at once undermines the principles upon which the rights of the individual rests. It neglects the fundamental notion that each man is responsible for his own wrongs, and that an officer acting beyond the limits of his constitutional authority is not an officer, but a personal trespasser. How shall we preserve "a government of law and not of men," if we cannot reach the officer who carries out an illegal act?

INDIVIDUALISM AND PRESENT PROBLEMS

At the beginning of the twentieth century we have come, in silence or in noisy disputation, consciously or unconsciously, to doubt some of the fundamental principles on which our institutions have rested. As I have already said, doubts have arisen in the minds of some, who appreciate the nature of our constitutional assumptions, as to whether it is possible for a modern state to do the work with which it is oppressed if it is to continue on a basis of individualism. In some particulars this question has arisen with regard to the application of criminal law. Our constitutional declarations were framed as the result of centuries of unjust and arbitrary treatment of the accused,

[1] See *Brooks* vs. *Mangan*, 86 Michigan 576.

when the government was supposed to be the enemy of the individual. In enforcing the constitutional privileges it sometimes appears as if the state had forgotten that it was quite as much its duty to convict the guilty as to protect the innocent. To the laymen there would seem to be no reason for the continuance of the individualistic atmosphere of criminal law in a country where crime is rampant, and where the accused, if arrested, finds opportunity to take advantage of numerous and unimportant technicalities—in a country where the law's delay is for the assistance of the predatory and the unsocial.

But more distinctly we have come to doubt whether men can do their duty to man if they are hemmed in by the restrictions of individualistic law. Those who work in the slums of the large cities and give their lives to elevating and comforting their fellow-men, who see the horrors of the tenement and the sweat shop, who come face to face with what misery can be wrought by the unbridled energy of avarice and selfish greed, demand now and again, with an energy that comes from conscientious conviction and whole-hearted devotion to right, restraints upon individual privilege of contract, and in reality demand a total surrender of the old-fashioned notion that one can do what one will with one's own. That such demands go too far many may believe; for, after all, the doctrine of the police power is now so widely developed that the state has the right, supported by decisions, to prohibit individual action or to restrain the personal right of contract, where action or agreement appear, in the opinion of legislatures and judges, to be distinctly detrimental to the public weal. Some of the recent decisions of the federal Supreme Court[1] declare that the police power extends to acts which are conducive to the convenience and prosperity of the community, and not simply to the prohibition of what may be distinctly detrimental to the public health or safety. On such an opinion as this the courts may, it appears, support any state law which would seem on its face conducive to the public well-being, and the old

[1] "In that case," says the Supreme Court of the United States, referring to the case of *C.B. & Q. R.R.* vs. *Illinois*, 200 U.S. 561, 592, "we rejected the view that the police power can not be exercised for the general well-being of the community. That power, we said, embraces regulations designed to promote the public convenience or the general prosperity, as well as regulations designed to promote the public health, the public morals, or the public safety."—*Bacon* vs. *Walker*, decided February 4, 1907 (Justice McKenna). Under this doctrine any interference with private conduct would be rightly regulated by legislation if it happened to strike the court as substantially helpful to the convenience of the community.

individualistic theory is reduced to a point of view from which to approach the consideration of a governmental act.

This proposition in its wider application has had to make way against all sorts of strenuous opposition, against learned briefs from able lawyers who base their arguments on old conditions, and who start with the old idea that the function of government is to keep the peace and allow individual initiative and individual right of contract full sway. Moreover, there has arisen constant necessity for watching narrowly this power of the state, for it is often invoked not for the common good, but for the supposed advantage of classes and cliques. If a law to limit the hours of work in bakeries, like that of New York recently passed on by the courts, has for its purpose, not the uplifting and protection of the health and well-being of the community, but the giving of advantage to a certain class of workmen without regard to rights and desires of the rest, or if it is merely an attack on an employer's right of contract, it can hardly be rightly supported as an exercise of the police power, which has in recent years made such inroads upon the notion of unrestrained individual struggle. This growth of the police power is a striking development of social rights in opposition to the assertiveness of unchecked individual privilege, and if the individualistic interpretation of our constitution and laws is to abide, it is because, by the exercise of the police power, a new principle of collectivism has become dominant and controlling in cases of a clear and absolute need. This principle of correction is antithetical to the doctrine of socialism in spite of its similarities; it proceeds on the notion of personal ownership and personal right of determination; but it controls individualism by considerations of public well-being and convenience, and, rightly applied, puts the interests of the state above the interests of any of its members.

In developing and applying the police power, the courts have had a new duty that has almost taken them from the field of law; and, if the power is to be rightly and effectively used, it would appear that time and again the judges must be guided, not by precedent, but by sense of substantial justice and by considerations which appeal rather to their intelligence as statesmen and wise humanists than to the learning of book-read lawyers. If the power is to be rightly and effectively used, I say, for by this route of encroachment on niggardly, selfish, personal greed, the state, the main body of the people, can reach, if it can at all, the popular care for the common well-being, without totally undermining in theory the principles of individualism underlying our laws and constitutions. It appears, indeed, that the courts and lawmakers, by one of those startling inversions that occur in human history, have been irresistibly called to grasp and promulgate a new doctrine of natural right—new, at least, as compared with the old doctrine of the independents, of Sam Adams and Thomas Jefferson —not the doctrine of the right existent in a state of nature, which existed before society, and for the protection of which society was established, but the right of substantial justice to society itself; and in the declaration of what government can do and what it cannot do, the sense of this right, like the old natural right, depends, when all is said, on a feeling for justice and not on humanly ordained law or statute. There is need once more to revert to the absolute as shown by the reason.

FEDERALISM AND LAW; RECENT CRITICISM

Within the last few years we have come almost to doubt the wisdom of the Fathers in trying to build up a great empire on the principle of law, in trying to form a great federal state where powers of government are distributed between the center and the parts, and in basing that distribution on a law unchangeable save through a combination and an effort difficult to attain. We have seen how out of our Revolutionary struggle came the states with constitutions recognized as law; and this legal foundation constitutes one of the two or three distinct contributions of the Revolution in its constructive aspect. There came into existence, too, a democratic empire founded on new principles. In the course of the Revolutionary argument certain characteristic differences of opinion between England and America showed themselves. In England the contention was for an empire with all power gathered at the center; all local power was to be exercised of grace and not of legal right. The Americans, in one form or another, demanded a legal empire, in which the localities, the states of the empire, should have their assured privileges, resting on no caprice of the central authority. After the Revolution two empires were in existence, both the products of English history; one was built on the principle that all legal power was at the center, however meagerly such power might be used, and that an empire could be reared under the guidance of opportunistic common sense and under the tutelage of justice. On this basis England has succeeded, and, following the lamp of experience and led on the whole by wisdom, has created and governed a stupendous empire. America's course has been different. Even before the Constitution was formed, her new colonial system was formulated in the famous Ordinance of 1787, which was fundamentally an unchanging law, as far as the opportunities of the time permitted or appeared to permit. When the Constitution was adopted, the new federal state came into existence, having for its most elementary idea the distribution of power between the center and the parts of a far-reaching democratic empire, a distribution made permanent by law and not to be varied by opportunistic reasoning or by appeals to temporary or eternal justice.

The continuance of a great federal organization, its bounds and partitions firmly marked by law, must depend on the accuracy with which that law distributes authority between the center and the parts. If the distribution is in accord with a mere temporary condition; if it does not leave to the states the powers that are there appropriately exercised; if it denies to the central government the control of subjects really general in character; if there is no proper room for local self-determination; or if, on the other hand, the impulses and desires of the great body of the people find themselves hampered by local obstinacy, local incompetence, or local selfishness and greed; if, in short, the distribution is not based on adequate and abiding justice and need, there is likely to arise conflict, disorder, uncertainty, and confusion—I do not mean that there will be war necessarily; but there will be the jolting, jarring, and rumbling of ill-adjusted machinery, the presence of political disorders which suggest inappropriateness of governmental system.

The effort to continue uninterruptedly in accord with a federal Constitution drawn up in days of individualism, and distributing authority between the government and the states, a Constitution made at a time when the states were living in comparative isolation, before the railroad, before the telegraph, before the thousand and one changes that have broken down state barriers in fact and welded us in reality, if not in law, into one mass in many social and vital particulars—the effort to continue uninterruptedly on the basis of such a law has produced difficulties and demanded numerous adjustments. These adjustments have been made easy in part by the general terms in which the Constitution of the United States is framed, making it unnecessary to follow literally the ideas that were present in the minds of its framers, who could not of course foresee one-hundredth of the future development or imagine even faintly its meanings. The only vital changes made in the Constitution by formal amendment since its beginning have been directed to lessening the competence of the state, not to increasing the vigor or the legislative scope of the national government. It is a striking fact, that, even if the states are now declared to be, because of their spatial limitations and their legal limits, unfit for undertaking new duties which have been brought about by the national expansion of industry, the state constitutions have been frequently amended to adapt them to new phases of thought and new needs. They are today almost the best indications of change of public conditions in the last hundred years, while the Constitution of the United States has been altered but once radically, and then for the purpose of calling in national power to *restrain* state activity, not to increase its own legislative competence. Were it not for the Fourteenth Amendment, there would today be almost nothing the state could not do through its constitution in disregard of individualistic doctrine.

Can our elastic federal Constitution, framed under conditions so different from those now existing, continue to be respected, in so far as it limits the competence of Congress? Many things have been done in the past and are done daily that are so far in advance of any conception of the Fathers, that we find difficulty, by processes of devious ratiocination, in reconciling them with the idea that the Constitution is a document of enumerated powers. But these changes have come slowly, and we have thought that we were still clinging tenaciously to the principle of law and the theory of constitutional limitation. Now, however, we are frankly told that the great fact of a national conscience, national will, and a national need must be recognized; if the states cannot individually do their duty, it will be done for them. This frank statement is not, as I conceive it, a threat, at least not a declaration of any imperious purpose to disregard the law or arrogantly to sweep state rights into the muck heap. It is an honest, clear-headed avowal of a very evident social truth: state negligence, state incompetence, state selfishness will not be permitted to stand in the way of overpowering national desire and a demanding national conscience; to say so is only to speak plainly what students of history know. The preservation of state rights depends, as ever, on the performance of state duties. If local self-government, as exemplified by the state capacity for self-management, is still of value, it must be maintained by unselfish devotion to right and justice.

In some particulars it may be that the nation will assume powers simply because they cannot be exercised by the states. We may find the national government taking charge of all trade and industry; we may see a law compelling all corporations engaged in commerce to reorganize under a federal charter; we may discover that insurance is commerce and that insurance companies doing business outside of a single state are forced to accept national regulations. We may, moreover, find other powers assumed by the national government because the states do not exercise considerately the powers they have; we may conclude that no individual state should be allowed to create trusts as a business, and that manipulation of securities is subject to national control. We may think that state marriage and divorce laws must not be made without consideration for the beliefs (and shall I say the rights?) of the people of other states. We may exercise the national power to prohibit child labor in local factories.

But it should be noticed that in all this there are several serious dangers. In some way we often go on the supposition that the federal authority is not of ourselves, but something apart and above our impulses; and this is simply destructive of the spirit of self-government. If the people of the state are on the whole derelict about duties that *can* be performed through local law, can we have assurance that the authorities at Washington will be superior to unwholesome influence and incompetence? Much of the demand for national interference comes from a curious unreasoning dualistic conception, as if the national government were a power disassociated from the people of the state, and as if the people of the United States were not also the people of the states. We forget also that because of our complicated system of checks and balances, because of an administrative system without ministerial responsibility, and because of political parties with a tremendous organization almost unknown to the law, national action can with great difficulty be made responsive to popular mandates.

I cannot refrain from pointing out also what everybody must have thought of—the danger that comes from a conscious disregard of law. If the national government in answer to a real national need can assume powers that are not granted, not only shall we lose local autonomy in considerable measure and surrender to that degree our conception of a federal state; but we shall consciously give up the idea of a law-abiding state and enter once again upon a government of men and not of law; we shall revert, in other words, to the condition against which the Fathers struggled and against which the forces of liberty were arrayed for centuries in English history. If the federal government can under pressure reach beyond its legal competence to do things for the state, there cannot in logic be an end; the very framework of government itself may be warped and broken under the pressure of opportunism and exigency. It is easy enough to argue that a president can go beyond his constitutional limits because he can act more expeditiously than a cumbersome Congress. Even now, at least one able, influential, and thoughtful journal (I do not mention the hare-brained variety) is demanding "centralized democracy," which is a euphemism for consolidated government and centralized authority. But from the highest point of view, can there be any greater danger than the conscious breach of confining law, unless it arises from the hypocritical pretense of regard for law, while one is consciously going beyond its limits? Have we reached that stage in our fretting against the bars of legal federalism?

TWO FUNDAMENTALS UNDER CRITICISM

It is strange, then, I may say in conclusion, that the two fundamentals that were striven for so long, the two great ideas which were imbedded in our constitutions, and which appeared to make them the lasting resting-place of permanent principles, the product of centuries of discussion and combat, are now in especial peril. To say the least, we are looking at them critically and pondering their value. Have we outgrown the idea of essential individualism with which our constitutions are impregnated, and the great idea of building up a competent federal republic, not on opportunism or a temporary view of justice, but on law?[1]

[1] It should, of course, be noticed that this was the essence of the Philippine question. The judge that announced the doctrine on which the government of the Philippines rests, in a later case declared that Congress is limited in its management of the territories only by natural rights. Brown, J., in *Rasmussen* vs. *U.S.*, 197 U.S. 516, 531. This, it is true, was the early contention of the

It was a saying, I believe, of Castelar, that man is free when he has to obey no one save the law. We may stop to question whether we really are free when we see that we are compelled to shape our actions by all sorts of men that prey upon the community. But we may add to this the saying, that liberty exists under government when there is a standing law to live by; and this, which is of course the elemental American idea woven into our constitutions, means that, if we have liberty, government itself must be the slave of law. Are we ready in studied advertence or by conscious frank design to abandon this principle?

Edmund Burke, the wise and philosophic friend of America, in one way heralded the successful British empire and ridiculed the idea, on which as a matter of fact the Americans reared the mighty fabric of a great imperial republic. He cast aside the notion of unchangeable law, and of abstract legal right as the foundation of political action: "The spirit of practicability, of moderation, and mutual convenience will never call in geometrical exactness as the arbitrator of an amicable settle-

American colonists against Great Britain; but we should notice that the outcome of their contention was the establishment of a government strictly confined by law.

ment." Let us notice, however, that this Titan among eighteenth-century statesmen also declared: "I feel an insuperable reluctance in giving my hand to destroy any established institution of government upon a theory, however plausible it may be."

INDEX

INDEX